AF241566

GET COACHING CLIENTS NOW

15 Step-by-Step STRATEGIES To Get High Paying Clients Quickly and Easily

CANDY MOTZEK

HOW TO BECOME A LIFE COACH AND START YOUR OWN BUSINESS

TABLE OF CONTENTS

FORWARD

My name is Candy Motzek, and I am an experienced coach, business mentor, and author. My clients are coaches, consultants, and entrepreneurs just like you! They've got topnotch training and are driven to make a difference in their clients' lives. The only problem is... they can have a hard time getting traction.

Sadly, many lifestyle entrepreneurs never make a profit and quickly find themselves on borrowed time. No clients mean no revenue. Overwhelmed with the burden of responsibilities weighing upon their shoulders, they feel overwhelmed and stuck, perhaps even trapped. Eventually most will give up on their hopes and dreams of building a successful coaching practice.

The world needs coaches. Why?

One, to help individuals break through barriers of limitation. Two, to support people as they overcome obstacles and as they grow so they can rise to their highest potential. In other words, the world doesn't just need coaches. The world needs *you* to be a coach!

Nothing makes me sadder than when a wonderfully talented practitioner walks away from their dream, walks away from their *calling*, because they were unable to make a profit — a scenario I once came dangerously close to myself.

Years ago, when completing my basic coaching training, I was pumped and primed! I dreamt of quitting my corporate day job and building my own full time coaching practice. Having worked in the corporate sector for years, I had external success: a nifty title and a great salary. I had arrived!

Except... I wasn't happy.

Every promotion brought the potential to exert more influence and increase my income. Confident that climbing the corporate ladder was the key to creating a difference, I was certain a sense of fulfillment would accompany my advancements.

With every promotion I worked my butt off to exceed expectations and dazzle the company leaders. Yet I discovered the higher I scaled the corporate ladder, the more isolated I felt. In a twisted way, each promotion diminished my hopes to create positive change. Instead my influence was limited by the mandate of the executives and shareholders.

One day it was proclaimed that to satisfy their annual profit goal, I would have to lay off a vital part of my team.

This was not the influence I longed for.

My team was like family. I knew of their family lives, their struggles, their hopes and joys. How on earth could I sacrifice *any* of them? Just writing this brings back the anxious knot to the depths of my stomach.

Determined to protect the integrity of my team, I resisted the corporate directive. But it became abundantly clear: either team members would have to go, or I would.

Although I complied with the directive, I now knew that I needed to make a change. It was time to plan for a transition, and eventually I made the choice to leave because I realized that I would never be truly fulfilled in the corporate arena.

I decided to follow a lifelong dream to become a coach!

When I completed my coaching training, I was enthusiastic to embark on the next chapter of my career! Hope and possibility percolated within me. I was excited to get out there and make the world a better place!

To be accredited, I had to generate five paying coaching clients before the end of the first month. I was certain this would be easy!

But at the end of that thirty days, I had no clients.

Zero.

Devastated and embarrassed, I felt I had surely failed. Where had I gone wrong? What was I going to do? Deep in my heart I *knew* I was meant to be a coach, but if I didn't have clients, how could I possibly be fulfilling my destiny? Much less, how could I keep a roof over my head and food on the table!

Kindly the trainers extended me a one-month grace period to fill my calendar with the bare minimum.

This moment was my turning point. I decided to *never* be without clients again and explored a broad range of approaches to ensure I *always* had clients. Many worked. Many didn't.

This story is the reason I'm writing this book... First to encourage you and help you fulfill your dreams of being a successful coach. Second, to share with you what has worked for me and what continues to work for me. If I can save you frustration and help you fill your client roster faster, then I will have done what I set out to do.

It was this experience that led me to supporting emerging coaches, consultants, and service entrepreneurs. I know firsthand the struggle to secure your first paying client, and I know the uncomfortable stretch to continually generate new ones.

But I also know the incredible satisfaction of exceeding my own goals and establishing a thriving coaching practice!

I want you to know this same sense of satisfaction and victory.

Today I am privileged to influence and support others in their own coaching journey. I've spoken with hundreds of new coaches, and hands down, the most frequently asked question is: **"How can I get more clients?"**

My mission is to assist amazing and motivated people build successful businesses, explaining how to do it in a practical step-by-step way, and providing practical, tried-and-tested strategies to establish or expand their practices.

This book is designed for new coaches and lifestyle entrepreneurs, as well as those looking to up level their business. The strategies and tactics outlined can be easily implemented to create a steady flow of clients and maintain your income level.

While using these strategies be sure to access my Free Resources Library where you'll find bonus materials including templates, worksheets, and tracking forms. The strategies, combined with the tools, are an invaluable resource for expanding your practice.

https://bit.ly/2MDhoql

Thank you. Thank you for daring to heed your calling. Thank you for stepping up to share your talent with the world.

Here's to your wildest success!

Candy Motzek
Step Into Success Now
stepintosuccessnow.com

CHAPTER 1

BUT FIRST, MINDSET

Before we dive in, let's get one thing abundantly clear. Whether you have a waiting list, or you're just starting out and have no clients at all, **you are an amazing person! If you weren't, you would never have gone into this field in the first place.** You are brave, passionate, determined, and quite understandably probably a bit nervous, maybe even doubtful at times.

Our mindset consists of the thoughts we hold and the emotions we experience. This combination impacts our efforts as much as, and sometimes even more than, the specific actions we take. Attitude, both internal and external, is a critical aspect to your success. While this book provides excellent proven strategies to attract clients, your mindset will very much impact your individual results. Are you aware of your mindset?

Do you innately believe in the transformative power of coaching?

If so, it is important to shift beyond a sales mindset and embrace an attitude of service. I used to think promoting my services more than once would be considered pushy. I worried the potential clients thought I was trying to sell them something, and "selling" felt icky. That was a barrier. To correct it, I had to reframe it and recognize I am offering a *solution* to their problem! People have all sorts of problems they desperately want to solve. You aren't bugging them. You may very well be the solution they have been searching for—they just didn't know it! Don't do them the disservice of keeping yourself the world's best kept secret.

Share your message...

over and over...

share your message!

Don't get discouraged if others aren't as excited about your new venture as you are! Don't take it personally if people have yet to fully understand the services you provide. Remind yourself you don't have to be perfect! Above all, don't play the comparison game. You have a unique skillset, life experiences, and perspectives that only **YOU** can provide to a client! Don't underestimate your abilities!

Remember there are people less qualified than you, successfully doing the things they want, simply because they decided to believe in themselves. PERIOD. So why not you?

No matter what your level of experience, rest assured you can get clients! In fact, you can get all the clients you want!

For that matter, you can attract your ideal like-minded clients without resorting to any slick or icky marketing tactics.

Are you prepared to believe it?

Clarity, commitment, and consistency are paramount to your journey.

Be sure you are very clear about the goals you have for your coaching practice. Take the time to determine *exactly* what you want to create! It is important to establish a strong foundation. While it may seem contradictory, you'll make progress faster if you initiate slow, steady actions instead of haphazardly trying different strategies for brief periods of time.

You're not going to be a coach for only six months. Focus on your long-term goals and realize this is a long-term game. Be prepared to play it as such!

What I know from my own experience is that I was so excited to establish my own coaching practice that it was easy to focus on polishing my approach to perfection. But that's not how client relationships are generated. There comes a time when we have to take bold, albeit perhaps imperfect, action, whether we feel ready or not.

People don't know that you are not as skilled as you would like to be or as you will be in the future.

People don't know that you are not as confident as you appear.

However, your enthusiasm, passion, and level of commitment will be obvious. This is far more important than striving to develop a perfect approach.

Have faith and know that this IS possible for you!

Be sure to keep in mind that you are building a *profitable and sustainable* professional coaching practice, one with plenty of excellent clients that will pay you for years to come. Agreed?

Action Checklist:

- 📌 **Believe in yourself.**

- 📌 **Establish a solid foundation of clarity.**

- 📌 **Act before you feel ready.**

- 📌 **Share your message and enthusiasm with others.**

- 📌 **Take consistent daily action.**

CHAPTER 2
CLARITY

As a new coach it is important that you have as much clarity as possible before paving the road ahead of you. This spares you the frustration of false starts and having to repeat your previous efforts.

There are four aspects that need to be explored:

1. What specifically are you looking to build?

2. What size practice are you looking to create? How many clients do you want?

3. Who is your ideal client? Who do you want to work with?

4. How do you solve their problems? What will your coaching package(s) look like?

YOUR DESIRED EXPERIENCE

What do you want to experience as a coach?

Are you interested in supplementing, or completely replacing, your current salary?

Do you want to build a small but highly profitable side hustle?

How many clients are you looking to attract? Keep in mind that a new coach focusing on one-on-one sessions will want to maintain a roster of between five to twenty-five individual clients.

Be clear regarding your long-term vision *now* to map out specific actions to bring it to fruition!

Download your worksheet and work through it to create your vision.

YOUR IDEAL CLIENT

You likely have heard of target markets, defining your ideal client avatar, or creating your perfect customer profile. These are all phrases that mean the same thing: **Who is your ideal client?**

Many experienced businesses spend days and weeks researching their demographics. As a new coach, I recommend you begin by giving yourself a couple of hours to define your ideal client. Get started now; remember, you will be able to return to this exercise repeatedly as your business grows and evolves.

Ask yourself:

» What types of people do I most enjoy talking to?

» Who are the kinds of people I know I can help?

» Who are the types of people that are motivated to act and can pay for my services?

Don't pressure yourself to make perfect decisions right now—you can change your mind at any time! The important thing is to begin getting coaching clients. The more people you coach, the clearer you will become regarding your ideal client. It is an experiential process, a spiral that circles around repeatedly. The important thing is to *begin*!

YOUR IDEAL CLIENT'S CURRENT EXPERIENCE

It is important to clearly identify what your ideal client is currently experiencing, issues they are facing and the changes they yearn for.

This segment entails actively brainstorming and researching your ideal client and their experience. The information uncovered can be fine tuned throughout your career, allowing you to better hone your efforts.

Your clarity transmutes into power!

This is not a book to be read and contemplated. As you are about to experience, you will be prompted to take immediate action.

Ready...

Get set...

Let's go!

MIND MAPPING

1. Understand your ideal client.

Right now, carve out the time and space to explore who your ideal client is and what they are facing. No matter how tempting, don't fall down the bottomless research rabbit hole! Set a timer for sixty to ninety minutes to keep you focused and on track. You don't want to spend days and weeks on this task. Aim to make a quick start with a small amount of research. Make some educated guesses, or even better, speak to a couple of people who are similar to your ideal client and ask what their current struggles are.

Begin by making four quick columns on a page.

Column #1: Describe highlights of your ideal client's current experience. Write down all the things you imagine they are struggling with. If you're unsure, find out! What sorts of things are the people around you frustrated by, or what are they struggling with in their daily lives? What do they complain about?

Column #2: Jot down as many hopes and dreams of your ideal client that you can possibly imagine. What changes do you think they aspire to?

Column #3: Reflect on your own life experiences. Which of these experiences can you leverage? What issues can you support your ideal client with?

Column #4: Specifically write down how their life improves when the issue has been resolved.

Download your worksheet and work through it to understand your ideal client.

Now, choose three to five everyday problems you can help solve or goals of which you can easily support their achievement. Highlight the problems you've chosen on the worksheet.

2. What is the journey your client will experience?

Coaching is a journey in which your client moves beyond pain into fulfillment. Your goal is to highlight your client's experience, to focus on them and their "hero's journey" rather than spotlight what you can do.

As you continue to use the worksheet from the Free Resources Library, fill in the journey. On the left hand side of the timeline, describe your ideal client's current state. On the far right hand side, briefly describe their life once they've achieved the goal or resolved the issue. Next, outline the steps they must take to take that journey.

https://bit.ly/2MDhoql

Create a step-by-step summary which answers the following:

1. What will your client learn?

2. What will they put into practice?

3. What new perspectives will they gain?

4. What obstacles will they easily overcome?

5. How will they transform?

Visit the Free Resources Library to access a downloadable PDF to capture the valuable insights you uncover in this process! You are mining gold! You want somewhere consistent and easily accessible to store the information.

The results of your mind-mapping session are a key part of the next segment. Take the time to complete this step before proceeding.

CLARIFYING LOGISTICS

There are many ways to coach: in person, by phone, or video conference. I've used Skype, Zoom Video Conference, Facetime, even Facebook Messenger for video calls. All are easy and inexpensive methods to set up. All you need is strong internet.

https://bit.ly/2MDhoql

How you deliver the coaching experience is entirely your choice. Decide what you are most comfortable with and what allows you to deliver the most successful sessions.

Once you decide, you will have to clearly explain it to your new client. Many people have never worked with a coach before, and they trust you to help them.

If you choose to coach in person, keep in mind you will need a space to meet your client where you will have privacy. You may also have to travel to the coaching sessions. This extra coordination and travel time will need to be reflected in your rates.

ESTABLISH YOUR RATES

If you are unsure what to charge, begin by doing your research. What are other coaches in your area charging? Once you know the range, you can decide on a figure somewhere in the middle.

Practice saying your rate out loud to yourself in the mirror. If you feel relatively comfortable, that's an awesome sign!

If quoting the rate makes you intensely uncomfortable, slightly reduce the rate and say it aloud to your reflection again. How do you feel now?

While it's important not to devalue your services, it's also imperative you feel somewhat comfortable and can declare your rate with confidence. Otherwise you will unintentionally sabotage yourself. Remember, you can always increase your rates as you gain experience and confidence!

ACCEPTING PAYMENT

An important part of positioning yourself as a professional is being clear in advance how you process payments. Three quick and easy methods to begin with are PayPal, Stripe, and e-transfers. Avoid complications—tell your clients you expect payment ahead of time. Clients who have "skin in the game" are far more motivated to act!

Action Checklist:

- 📌 Define exactly the type of practice you want to create.

- 📌 Identify your ideal client.

- 📌 Mind map your ideal client's current experience.

- 📌 Choose three to five common problems you can help your client with.

- 📌 Access the downloadable PDFs in the Free Resources Library.

- 📌 Decide how you will deliver your coaching sessions.

- 📌 Establish your rates.

- 📌 Practice quoting your rate.

- 📌 Identify how to process payments.

https://bit.ly/2MDhoql

CHAPTER 3
NOW, GET READY

KNOW-LIKE-TRUST FACTOR

There is a concept called the "Know-Like-Trust" factor that you need to be aware of and leverage when building your clientele. It says that if any of these three components (know, like, or trust) are missing, your potential client will not buy and they will not sign up with you. Spend a few minutes reflecting on your own experiences. Have you ever happily purchased from a business or a business person that you didn't *like*? When you go out shopping, I bet you usually go to your favorite stores first, especially the shops where they *know* you and you *know* them. Notice too that if you personally don't *trust* the business or the individual you are potentially buying from, you will decline and go elsewhere.

If your potential clients don't trust you, they will not want to hire you as their coach because they won't feel comfortable talking about their issues and revealing their vulnerabilities in your presence.

When you are engaging a potential client, take time to genuinely build rapport. This will build your Know-Like-Trust factor and will help you sign up more clients.

YOUR SIGNATURE SENTENCE

It is crucial that you can confidently introduce yourself as a coach and quickly explain the services you provide. Your "Signature Sentence" does just that! It is a condensed description of how you help your clients. Shorter than the traditional elevator pitch, your Signature Sentence is no more than two lines and is able to be spoken in a single breath.

The results from your mind mapping session are a valuable part of crafting your Signature Sentence. If you have read ahead without delving into the brainstorming session, *go back and act before reading any further.* Taking action as you go is a key piece of establishing and expanding your business.

There are four components to your Signature Sentence:

1. Identify your niche.

2. Provide a common problem your clients face.

3. Highlight how life improves when the problem is resolved.

4. Declare you are looking for similar clients and ask for a referral.

Here are a couple of Signature Sentence examples for your consideration:

"I'm a career coach. I help people identify their dream career and secure high-paying employment with a minimum of stress. My roster has room for a few new clients. Who do you know that I can connect with?"

Or,

"I'm a parenting coach. I help parents and teenagers overcome conflict and bring the family together. I am looking for new clients. Who do you know that would benefit from my services?"

Included in the Free Resource Library is a downloadable worksheet to help you craft your Signature Sentence. Download it now and take twenty to thirty minutes to craft your own laser-focused blurb.

Once you've created your Signature Sentence, rehearse it until it feels completely natural and you're able to deliver it with confidence! Sharing your message repeatedly is crucial to promoting your services. Practice until it becomes habit. You are developing and strengthening your new client getting skillset.

Anytime you are introduced, share your Signature Sentence with your new acquaintance! Consistently sharing it with people you meet helps get your message visible.

https://bit.ly/2MDhoql

Share your Signature Sentence with:

» Friends and family

» New acquaintances

» Networking introductions

» When you are a guest blogger

» When being introduced on podcasts

» When introducing yourself on social media

Right now, go add your Signature Sentence and website link to the following:

» Your email signatures

» Your LinkedIn profile

» Your Twitter profile

» Your Instagram profile

» Your Pinterest profile

» Your personal Facebook profile

» Your Facebook business page

» The back of your business cards

Already you are taking action! Congratulate yourself on the steps you are taking.

Make it easy for people to understand exactly what you do, and make it ridiculously easy for them to reach you! The fewer barriers you have, the more people will reach out to you.

DEVELOP YOUR COACHING PACKAGES

In the Clarity segment, you were asked to identify how you would deliver your coaching sessions. This information is a cornerstone to developing your coaching packages.

The strategies and insights garnered in previous segments are building blocks for your development and expansion.

To design your coaching packages, you will need to decide the following:

1. Precisely how are your sessions structured?

2. What frequency of sessions will work best?

3. How long do you anticipate the coaching relationship to last?

You will want to structure your format, so your client can see tangible progress. Will that mean you connect with your client for thirty minutes each week or for sixty minutes every second week? How many coaching sessions will it take for your client to reap the benefits?

It is also important that your structure is accessible for a client to book. For example, it is easier to promote a package of six sessions rather than a six-month commitment. You will want to keep the sale as simple as possible. In time, you can progress and expand to offer a signature program. Until then, you want to ensure it is psychologically accessible to your prospective clients. Make it easy for people to hire you, and they will.

Action Checklist:

- ★ **Visit the Free Resources Library and download the Signature Sentence worksheet.**

- ★ **Craft your Signature Sentence.**

- ★ **Practice, practice, practice speaking your Signature Sentence aloud.**

- ★ **Share your Signature Sentence with family, friends, and acquaintances.**

- ★ **Add your Signature Sentence and website link to your email signature.**

- 📌 **Embed your Signature Sentence in the profiles of all your social media accounts.**

- 📌 **Introduce yourself confidently as a coach.**

- 📌 **Make it easy for everyone to understand exactly what you do.**

- 📌 **Make it ridiculously easy for people to contact you.**

- 📌 **Develop your coaching packages.**

- 📌 **Ensure the sale is psychologically accessible.**

- 📌 **Celebrate the action you are taking and find a way to reward your efforts.**

CHAPTER 4
GET PROACTIVE

When you were prompted to explore your desired experience as a coach, I hope you identified wanting a smooth experience. Every action taken today will contribute to your future experience.

What can you do *now* to ensure a peaceful experience? Proactive measures today will save you confusion, frustration, and being overwhelmed. Plus, it positions you as a confident coach capable of navigating an influx of new clientele!

If five clients landed in your lap today, would you be able to accommodate them?

Before obtaining new clients, you must be prepared to welcome them!

Avoid the pitfall of preparing to be in business. Opt for progress over perfection! And keep your approach simple and streamlined.

Let's explore what you can do now to ensure your desired experience while creating a profitable coaching practice:

» What sort of welcome or intake package will you implement?

» How will clients book sessions with you?

This part of your foundation can be completed in a matter of days. You don't want to risk falling into *perpetual preparation* to be in business, so it is important to set constraints on the amount of time spent on the following. No matter how tempting, don't become distracted by administrative "stuff," personal brand, or design aspects instead of generating clients. Focus on these basics as a launching pad from which you will jump into action!

INTAKE SYSTEM

As a new coach, you certainly don't need a slew of complicated paperwork. All you need to do is determine how you want to welcome your client. The only paperwork necessary is a welcome letter, a basic coaching agreement, a pre-coaching questionnaire, and a simple invoice.

I am a proponent of the KISS methodology: "Keep It Simple, Sweetie." Here is my recommended timeline for issuing components of the welcome package.

What to Send	When It's Sent
A Welcome Letter	Once they've committed to coaching
Your Invoice	Send it with the welcome letter
Thank you note that includes a link to your online scheduler	Once you've received payment
Basic Coaching Agreement and Pre-Coaching Questionnaire (to discuss on your first call and will help them get the benefits of coaching more quickly)	When they've set up their first coaching session

Decide to streamline your process even further right now!

Visit the Free Resources Library and access your 50% discount coupon to purchase a downloadable package including all the necessary forms!

https://bit.ly/2MDhoql

SCHEDULING

When I was a novice coach, it would often take three or more rounds of emails back and forth to finally establish a convenient time for a client session. Talk about a huge waste of time and effort! Coaching is not supposed to be frustrating—for you, or the client.

Online schedulers are a quick and easy solution!

Signing up with a scheduling provider gives you the ability to establish in advance the dates and times you are available to coach. Plug the options into your calendar and present the schedule to your client. By inserting the link directly into your emails, you have already begun to streamline your intake process, and in doing so you demonstrate professionalism from the very beginning.

Be sure to check out my Free Resources Library for an array of online scheduling software choices including many free options!

Action Checklist:

📌 **Visit the Free Resources Library for an array of online scheduling providers.**

📌 **Choose and implement one.**

📌 **Enter your availability in said software.**

📌 **Access the 50% discount coupon in Free Resources Library and purchase your downloadable Intake Package.**

CHAPTER 5
BOLD ACTION

Whether excitement or nerves, when there's a lot of emotion attached to an endeavour, there is a natural inclination to focus on all the little details. Planning and polishing can easily become an effective distraction from doing the actual work of recruiting clients.

Give yourself permission to take action <u>before</u> you feel ready, so you can avoid falling into the trap of perpetually "getting ready."

Consistent daily action will yield results!

I love the story of how Jerry Seinfeld started in comedy as recalled by interviewer Brad Isaac.

> *Jerry explained the way to be a better comic was to create better jokes. The way to create better jokes was to **write every day**. But his advice was better than that! He had a gem of a leverage technique he used on himself, and you can use it to motivate yourself—even when you don't feel like it! He revealed a unique calendar system he used to pressure himself to write. Here's how it works.*

Brad Isaac goes on to share...

He said to get a big wall calendar that has a whole year on one page and hang it on a prominent wall. The next step was to get a big red magic marker.

He said for each day that I do my task of writing, I get to put a big red X over that day.

After a few days, you'll have a chain. Just keep at it, and the chain will grow longer everyday. You'll like seeing that chain, especially when you get a few weeks under your belt. Your only job next is not to **break the chain!**

Don't break the chain, he said again for emphasis.

Jerry's experience is a powerful testimony of amazing results generated by commitment to consistent daily action.

No matter where you are on your professional coaching path—whether you are in pursuit of your first paid client, or if you are looking to expand an existing practice—consistent daily actions are the most influential factor of your success!

Action Checklist:

- 📌 **Identify specific daily steps.**

- 📌 **Commit to consistent daily action.**

- 📌 **Determine how you will track your efforts.**

- 📌 **Don't break the chain.**

CHAPTER 6
SAMPLE SESSIONS

"Sample Session" is a term I will be using throughout this book. It is your opportunity to show a potential client the valuable experience of coaching. Sample Sessions can be conducted face-to-face, over the telephone, or via video conferencing.

Sample Sessions are complimentary consultations for qualified prospects. By "qualified prospects," I mean: someone who is likely to pursue coaching; someone that represents your ideal client; someone who has issues you can help alleviate; and also importantly, someone who can pay for your services.

Be selective with your prospective clients. I know you're eager to get paying clients, but it is important to listen to your gut and trust your intuition. This may seem contradictory—me writing a book on how to gain clients, then advising that you be selective. But the truth is, if your gut is telling you "not this one," you likely will not enjoy working with them. They may turn out to be more trouble than the effort is worth.

Back to Sample Sessions... I cannot emphasize this enough: Sample Sessions are NOT free coaching.

A Sample Session is an exploratory conversation to help a qualified prospect decide if they would like to hire you as their coach, and at the same time, for you to decide if you would like to be their coach.

There is a big difference between giving your service away for free, and helping the client identify the problem and envision the solution. The point is to help them recognize precisely how you can assist them and clearly identify the benefits of hiring you.

Think about it... if you provide a complimentary coaching session, the recipient will leave the conversation feeling better. There will be no incentive to hire you. They won't immediately recognize that lasting results are achieved by an ongoing coaching relationship.

Remember: Always send confirmation twenty-four hours before your scheduled Sample Sessions!

SAMPLE SESSION STRUCTURE

Have a defined structure you follow during your Sample Sessions. This does not mean a script, but rather specific touchpoints so you are confident you will cover everything.

My Sample Sessions follow this structure:

1. Introduction

2. Understand the Problem

3. Demonstrate Perspective

4. Identify the Gap

5. Explore the Benefits

6. Explain How They Can Hire You

7. Wrap It Up

8. Follow Up

INTRODUCTION:

It is important that the Sample Session client be encouraged to relax. Most people don't know what coaching is, and so they may be nervous. Create rapport, and ask them questions to help them feel comfortable, e.g.:

"Where are you from?"

"What do you do for work?"

"How did you find me?"

UNDERSTAND THE PROBLEM:

You want to find out about what they want to achieve.

Ask them:

"What's been getting in your way lately?"

"What's been going on in your life that you would like to resolve?"

"What are you experiencing difficulties with right now?"

The goal is to specifically understand their problem and how it is affecting every aspect of their life. Once they've described the situation, follow up with:

"How is this affecting you?"

"What is a specific way this problem hinders you?"

"What have you done to try and solve this so far?"

DEMONSTRATE PERSPECTIVE:

Now is the time to help them gain perspective on their issue. What are the facts? What is going on with their thinking and emotions surrounding the issue? Help them to recognize that their thoughts are affecting their emotions, which in turn impacts their actions and reactions.

"Where else does this show up in your life?"

Our issues are not isolated. Help them see how an issue affects more than one aspect of life. This lays the groundwork that a solution will have a beneficial ripple effect throughout their life. Help them paint the picture of how life will be when the issue is rectified by asking:

"What would be possible if the problem was solved?"

"What would your life be like?"

"How would you feel?"

"What would you be able to do differently?"

"What new and exciting opportunities would be available to you?"

Much of the coaching experience is you asking powerful, curious questions and allowing them to consider their replies.

IDENTIFY THE GAP:

At this point, the two of you have explored the difference between where they currently are versus where they could be. Their problem is clear, and together you've begun exploring a potential and hopeful future.

This is the time to explain how coaching bridges the gap.

**Explain how your coaching program will
help them.**

EXPLORE THE BENEFITS:

Highlight how the benefits of the program will transform the client's emotional experiences.

For example, a coach specializing in self-confidence may say, "After coaching, you'll find you no longer feel stuck. Your clarity and confidence will have improved! You'll have gained new practical skills easily applicable to your life. You'll have the tools to be more comfortable asking for a promotion. You'll show up more powerfully in life! You'll be able to make small talk with people you've just met."

EXPLAIN HOW TO HIRE YOU:

After explaining the benefits of your coaching program, present the price and logistics of the sessions. For example: "We will have a forty-five-minute session every week for twelve weeks. I will also provide handouts and audios you can access between sessions. I am also available for email support. The investment is $______________."

Respond to any questions or concerns they raise using the same helpful collaborative tone maintained throughout the Sample Session. Don't kick it into sales gear.

Remember, you are helping them understand how coaching will benefit their life, and at the same time determining if you'd like to work with them!

WRAP IT UP:

"How does that sound?"

"When shall we begin?"

"If you signed up for this program, what would you like to have happen in the next twelve weeks? When that happens, how will your life feel?"

I bet your sample session has gone well! Now they sound excited too. What do you do when they are ready to get started? Well, I recommend if they are ready to commit, pull out your calendar and book their first session right away. Don't delay! Clients tend to second guess themselves once they've returned to their currently normal, albeit somewhat unsatisfying, life because it is what they are used to. So, get that first coaching call booked and confirmed.

FOLLOW UP:

If your potential client is not yet ready to make the commitment, follow up with them periodically. Most client engagements are signed because of friendly, helpful follow-up.

PRACTICE DELIVERING SAMPLE SESSIONS:

Ask a friend to play the role of your ideal client. Have your Sample Session structure in front of you as you practice ensuring you hit the significant milestones.

Give your partner a list of objectives and ask them to offer their own too.

Remind yourself—you don't have to be perfect!

Repeatedly practice explaining the benefits of the coaching program, explaining how they can hire you, and master wrapping up the sale.

When I first began coaching, I delivered what I knew were awesome Sample Sessions. But at the last minute, I would get nervous and not ask for the business. Give yourself permission to be a beginner; just make sure to learn from your mistakes and keep improving.

The more you practice, the more comfortable and confident you will feel!

TELL YOUR PEOPLE:

Talking to people is what matters, and truthfully, people don't know that you're not as skilled as you will be in the future. Instead they will hear your excitement! Besides, the level of commitment and passion you bring is more important than getting it perfect.

Tell your people that you are actively accepting new clients. Tell them there is room in your schedule. Tell them you offer complimentary Sample Sessions.

Share your message. Over and over. Share your message!

Don't be the world's best kept secret.
Tell your people!

CHAPTER 7

TRACKING + ACTION =TRACTION

We have all seen a vehicle stuck in the snow, unable to get traction, spinning its wheels and making the rut deeper. You have places to go on this amazing journey of yours. Make sure you have adequate traction!

Tracking our efforts is a key factor to consistent daily action! It keeps us accountable in our efforts, reflects our progress, and builds momentum. It also provides valuable research as to what's working and what's not.

**Jerry Seinfeld put an X through every day he wrote.
How will you track your daily efforts?**

Our most recent memories are the strongest, especially when tied to strong emotions!

We easily forget what happened a month ago. When our actions are measured objectively and physically tracked, we avoid falling into a skewed perspective. At the same time, we gain profound insight as to what's working and can better invest our energy!

Uncover the best uses of your strategy and investment of energy—head over to the Free Resources Library and download your tracking sheet!

Action Checklist:

- 📌 **Who will you tell today that you are a coach? Remember your Signature Sentence!**

- 📌 **What will your daily quota be for the number of people you share your message with?**

- 📌 **Who will you ask to practice Sample Sessions with you?**

- 📌 **Establish a weekly goal of Sample Sessions you wish to facilitate.**

- 📌 **Send confirmations of Sample Sessions twenty-four hours beforehand.**

- 📌 **How will you track the Sample Session invitations you have issued?**

- 📌 **Who will you ask for referrals?**

📌 **If you haven't already, download the tracking template from the Free Resources Library.**

📌 **Continue taking consistent daily action.**

📌 **Continue tracking all your efforts.**

📌 **Celebrate the progress you are making!**

CHAPTER 8

THE ASK

Asking for business is the vital link between looking for clients and having clients! To get more clients, you must ask more people. It's *that* simple.

In marketing they refer to "The Rule of 7" which says that you will need to share your message with a potential client seven times before they buy from you.

Society deals with a lot of noise; we are constantly bombarded with marketing messages. In turn we try to tune a lot of these advertisements out because they are so overwhelming. It's like wearing earplugs in a factory—you'll hear some things, but not everything.

It's no different with potential ideal clients. They're not sitting around waiting for you to show up—they're busy living their lives. You may not even be a blip on their radar—*yet*. They don't need you right now, so they don't notice you. *Yet.*

You need to consciously decide to share your Signature Sentence and ask for the business. This must become a number one priority!

It may not be exactly seven times before your message registers, but this is information to be considered!

You must tell people what you are doing, and specifically tell them you are looking for clients. If it doesn't register with them the first time, don't worry. Tell them again! They may not have heard you. So, ask them again.

You can pursue all the right strategies and be completely prepared to coach, but if you never *ask* for the business, you will remain stuck and clientless.

While it may seem obvious when you're reading this, you'd be surprised the amount of new coaches who deliver amazing Sample Sessions, but freeze when it's time to declare, "When would you like to start?" Remember, it happened to me too!

Don't chicken out at the last minute

Your goals are ahead of you. Move towards them. Ask for the business!

Coaching is a valuable service, one that supports individuals to overcome their issues and create a better life. You owe it to them to give them the opportunity to experience the benefit of a coaching relationship with you. If you don't ask for the business, you are doing a grave disservice to both of you. If you don't coach them, they could remain stuck forever!

If you don't ask, and don't ask regularly, you cannot expect to receive. Do not be afraid to call people to action!

Give them the opportunity to work with you. Ask them to. You'll be surprised with the response.

TRANSFORMING "NO" INTO "NOT YET"

We are conditioned to hear the word "no" and perceive it as rejection. I know when I used to hear it, I thought it was a red light at which I was to stop and not go any further.

Your success will be contingent on reframing this assumption.

Many times, you may ask someone if they would like to begin coaching, and they will reply with "no." Since we never really know what someone else is thinking, or what is going on in their life at that immediate moment, "no" could mean any number of things. Let's explore this.

When a potential client says:

It might mean this instead:

Not yet.
I'm not sure it will work for me.
I'm not ready to work on this.
I don't entirely understand
How coaching will help me.
I don't know you well enough yet to trust you.

When you hear the word "no," don't let your inner critic run wild. Do not doubt your ability to be a successful coach. If it is possible for others to grow a satisfying profitable coaching business, then you can too! It is how we respond to that "no" that impacts our potential success.

When you decide the word "no" is the end of your discussion	When you decide the word "no" is the mid-point of your discussion
Invite them to a Sample Session.	Invite them to a Sample Session.
Book the date.	Book the date.
Get together and explore their issues or goals.	Get together and explore their issues or goals.
Explain how coaching will help them.	Explain how coaching will help them.
Show them how coaching will help them.	Show them how coaching will help them.
Ask what they think.	Ask what they think.
Accept their objections, thank them, and walk away.	Get curious and coach the objections/ concerns they raise.
Feel disappointed because your bank account and calendar are empty.	Again, show them how much their life will improve because of coaching.

Delete their contact information because they said "no."	Invite them to begin. When would you like to begin? When shall we book our first session?
Start from square one again and find another person for a Sample Session.	If they do not sign up, continue to nurture the relationship. Many will join later.

If you have a good conversation with a prospective client and you'd like to coach them, continue investing in the relationship. Send them the occasional note or article you think they'd like. Ask them if you can add them to your email list and send occasional correspondence. Continue adding value to their life. Continue being present.

You never know when they may be in a better spot to begin coaching. They will have appreciated the consideration you have demonstrated, and once again you have invested in the "Know-Like-Trust" factor.

Action Checklist:

- ✪ Remember the Marketing Rule of 7 and be persistent.

- ✪ Extend invitations to experience a Sample Session.

- ✪ Specifically ask for recommendations.

- ✪ Add Sample Session invitations to your email signature.

- ✪ Embrace your Signature Sentence.

- ✪ Establish a weekly goal of how many Sample Sessions you will facilitate.

- ✪ Track all invitations and schedule for future follow-up.

- ✪ Be mindful of your internal dialogue. Don't let the Inner Critic stop you.

★ Transmute "no" into "not yet," and schedule for future correspondence.

★ Update all social media profiles to announce "I am accepting new clients. PM me to learn more!"

SUCCESS STRATEGIES

15 *PROVEN* CLIENT-GENERATING TACTICS

STRATEGIES

Some of the strategies I offer are easy, others more complex. All of them are low or no cost which makes them easily attainable for new business owners on a tight budget.

Time and time again my clients have proven that when these strategies are put into practice, they quickly yield results!

Begin by selecting a couple of methods to embed within in your business plan. Experiment to see which are your favorites, and then—lather, rinse, and repeat!

In this section we will be exploring the following proven strategies for success:

Strategy #1:   **Who Do You Know? Leverage Your Contact**

Strategy #2:   **Follow Up with Finesse**

Strategy #3:   **Leverage Referrals**

Strategy #4:   **Launch with A Bang!**

Strategy #5:   **Facebook**

Strategy #6:   **Get Face-to-Face**

Strategy #7:   **Volunteer**

Strategy #8:   **Craigslist**

Strategy #9:   **Create a Business Referral Network**

Strategy #10:   **Initiate a Coaching Collective**

Strategy #11:   **Deal Sites**

Strategy #12:   **Host a Workshop**

Strategy #13: Deliver a Signature Speech

Strategy #14: Host a Public Event

Strategy #15: Become the Kind of Coach You Yourself Would Hire

STRATEGY #1:
WHO DO YOU KNOW? LEVERAGE YOUR CONTACT LIST

This strategy works best when approached methodically and systematically. It will help you quickly fill your schedule with paying clients and net you a steady stream of future clients. It is a low-cost method that only requires your time and dedication. Since you are pursuing warm leads, it requires less time than cold calls. The beauty of this system? It is repeatable and can be easily used anytime you desire an influx of new clients.

Begin by making a list of everyone you know. Include their name, all phone numbers, mailing address, and email address.

This will likely be a long list, so I recommend doing it electronically. Use software such as Customer Relationship Management software (CRM), Excel, Evernote, or Pages. I prefer to create my lists in Excel because I can quickly sort, format, and track the results.

I've created a downloadable spreadsheet available in the Free Resources Library, and all you have to do is fill in the blanks.

https://bit.ly/2MDhoql

Name	Email Address			
Mary Richardson	mr@gmail.com			
Ian Lee	IL123@live.com			
John Brown	JBrn@gmail.com			
Jane Fuller	jane@gmail.com			
Cindy Char	IL123@live.com			
June Smith	Js@gmail.com			

Make an initial list of friends, family members, and peers that immediately come to mind.

Supplement this list by reviewing your phone contacts and email accounts. Then review social media accounts such as LinkedIn, Facebook, and Instagram. Don't forget to include the stack of business cards you've collected! Remember to include all the people you currently work with, and those you've worked with in the past. Include people you've done volunteer work with, previous neighbours, and other past acquaintances.

Begin by adding *everyone* to your list!

Keep this list active; update it anytime you meet new people.

The goal of your master list is quantity, not quality. Paring the list down is an upcoming piece of this strategy.

Next to each name place a reminder of where you know them from. Complete this step for each contact on your list.

Name	Email Address	How Do We Know Each Other
Mary Richardson	mr@gmail.com	Worked at ABC Co.
Ian Lee	IL123@live.com	University
John Brown	JBrn@gmail.com	Family
Jane Fuller	jane@gmail.com	Worked at ABC Co.
Cindy Char	IL123@live.com	University
June Smith	Js@gmail.com	Referral

After each descriptive reminder is identified, review the list asking yourself if you "Know-Like-Trust" them, and do they "Know-Like-Trust" you?

Here are the three examples so you can see how to use this rating system:

			Know-Like-Trust
Mary	I like and trust her	She doesn't like or trust me	No
Mary	I don't like or trust her	She likes and trusts me	No
Mary	I like and trust her	She likes and trusts me	Yes

Chances are if you Know-Like-Trust them, the feeling is mutual. And conversely, if the Know-Like-Trust factor is not present for you, it very well may not be for them either.

Review your list and classify the people on it based on whether you think they may be highly interested, moderately interested, or disinterested in coaching.

I would give them a number grade like this:

Highly interested = 1, Moderately interested = 2, Disinterested = 3

Name	Email Address	How Do We Know Each Other	Interest Level
Mary Richardson	mr@gmail.com	Worked at ABC Co.	1
Ian Lee	IL123@live.com	University	1
John Brown	JBrn@gmail.com	Family	2
Jane Fuller	jane@gmail.com	Worked at ABC Co.	1
Cindy Char	IL123@live.com	University	3
June Smith	Js@gmail.com	Referral	1

Filter your list for all people who have "yes" down for the Know-Like-Trust factor AND those you've classified as #1 (highly interested).

**Congratulations! You made great progress.
This is the initial group of contacts you will invite to a
Sample Session!**

To clarify how this strategy works using the above example:

1. June Smith, Jane Fuller, and Mary Richardson would be the first people you approach.

2. John Brown would be in the second wave of people to approach.

3. Cindy Char would be in the third wave of people.

4. You will not contact Ian Lee.

Send a personalized email or handwritten note to each of them. The most powerful approach is to write the handwritten note. The impact you will have on potential clients will be profound even in this day and age. Take heed: this is not a copy and paste mass approach. Each note will include:

» A brief greeting.

» If it's been a while since you spoke, include a reminder of where you know one another from.

» Ask about something you remember about them.

» Tell them about your new coaching venture.

» Invite them to a Sample Session.

» Tuck in two of your business cards—one for them and one to share with a friend.

Here's a sample:

> *Hi Sarah,*
>
> *I hope you are well! How are your kids? Sammy must be entering high school soon! I'm always amazed at how fast our kids grow up!*
>
> *I've started a new venture as a work-life balance coach! I'm really excited about it and wanted to share the news with you.*
>
> *Most of my clients are Type-A Overachiever Moms struggling to find the balance between their career ambitions and caring for their family. I know we've talked about this in the past, so I wanted to reach out to you. I'd love to explain more about my coaching and offer you a small demonstration as I'm looking for ways to grow my business.*
>
> *If you're interested I'd love to talk with you and have a Sample Session so you can experience it for yourself.*
>
> *I look forward to hearing from you.*
>
> *Katherine*

> *P.S. Most of my clients come through referrals. If you know someone who would benefit from coaching, please send them my way for a free Sample Session.*

By taking the time to connect with those in your network, you are building on your existing relationships and can invite people to experience a Sample Session. Be sure to include your Signature Sentence so they know the types of people with whom you are looking to work.

Send one to three notes everyday instead of trying to tackle 500 customized notes in one week.

In your Customer Relationship Management software or tracking sheet, keep close track of:

» The people you've reached out to (remember to invite them to a Sample Session!).

» The date you sent the note.

» When you are scheduled to follow up.

Scheduling your follow-up on this is crucial!

If you haven't heard back from them in seven days, send them a follow-up email. People are busy and distracted. A friendly follow-up bumps you back to the top of their inbox. Include another invitation to a Sample Session, and be sure to ask them who they know that would be a good fit to experience a Sample Session.

If you don't get a response from this second email, mark your schedule to follow up with them again in a month or two. You may have caught them at a bad time. It could be worth a third email in the coming months to continue the relationship.

When the time has passed, send them a follow-up and let them know how well your business is growing. Remind them of how much you enjoyed connecting with them in the past, and you are always approachable if they decide they are interested in a Sample Session in the future or if they have someone they can refer.

Even if your business is overflowing with clients, do not avoid sending the follow-up. These people are your best options to grow your client base since you already have a relationship them. It can be a very productive and satisfying way to grow your business.

Be sure to track:

» Who replies

» Who books a Sample Session

» Who sends you referrals, and the names of the people referred

After tracking the data for a few weeks, you will be able to predict the efficiency of your approach. If you book a Sample Session for every ten emails you send and secure a paying client for every three Sample Sessions you conduct, you are inspired to continue with your efforts and keep on keeping on!

Remember to download your free copy of the master tracking sheet from the Free Resources Library.

Action Checklist:

- 📌 **Visit my Free Resources Library and download the contact list spreadsheet.**

- 📌 **Complete the spreadsheet utilizing all fields (where you know them from, Know-Like-Trust, and the evaluated level of interest in coaching).**

- 📌 **Send a custom personalized message.**

- 📌 **Record the date of your message.**

- 📌 **Schedule to follow up.**

- 📌 **Set a goal to send out one to three emails to people from the initial subset contact list every day.**

- 📌 **Set your plan in motion and stay dedicated and consistent.**

- 📌 **Schedule to review again in three months.**

- 📌 **Track all messages, replies, and responses.**

STRATEGY #2:
FOLLOW UP WITH FINESSE

Every step, every action, every strategy requires follow-up and attention. Following up with finesse is strategy #2, and it can be incorporated with every strategy that follows from here.

Follow-up is a crucial part of any action. Otherwise, it will seem you are taking all the right steps to grow your client base, but your business won't be growing as fast as you'd like. When you increase the frequency and quality of your follow-up, you may find it's the missing link necessary to skyrocket your success.

Here's what I mean ... many coaches will do an awesome Sample Session and consistently ask the potential client when they would like to begin coaching. When the response is "not right now," a coach may hesitate to follow up. It's easy to get nervous and think you are bugging them or that you are being too pushy.

Two of the most frequently asked questions I get from my clients are:

"When should I follow up?"

"How do I do it?"

Let's begin by reframing your perspective. You may feel you are bugging them, or that you are acting like an aggressive door-to-door salesman. When you are deeply anchored in the profound value coaching brings people and pursue your follow-up from a place of genuine service, not only will you feel better about following up, but the prospective client will sense that positive energy. They will know you are coming from a place of genuine caring and kindness.

Statistics show that 80% of sales occur after seven attempts!

Yet most people give up after only two. This means that most coaches are missing out on prospective clients who would have likely signed up... if only they had continued to build the relationship.

There is a lot of noise and distraction in our world. Following up increases the odds of what you're offering being recognized. You must break through the static of surroundings with a consistent, repeated message.

More follow-up means more clients, which means fewer Sample Sessions and less seeking on your part. Following up with individuals who have already experienced a Sample Session with you will result in a more vibrant coaching practice with more clients.

Here's how a typical conversation might go between a coach and a potential client.

Coach: "Would you like to start coaching?"

Client: "No thanks, not yet."

Two weeks later...

Coach: "How about now? Are you ready to start coaching?"

Client: "I'm really busy these days. Now is just not a good time."

Conversation over.

But now you know that most clients sign up after *seven contacts!* No longer will you miss out by dropping the lead after a mere two attempts.

So, when is the best time for you to follow up? And what is the best way for you to do so?

The quick answer is that each potential client is different. Some will want to hear from you next week by phone. Others will want to hear from you next month by email. How will you know which is which?

The easiest way is for you to be direct and ask them during you Sample Session.

Once you've established they are not ready for coaching just yet, ask them these two questions:

"When shall I follow up with you?"

"What is the best way for me to connect with you?"

They will tell you exactly what's right for them. Once you know that, you can add a reminder to your calendar. When the time comes, follow up with them in the way they have asked, i.e., respect the follow up method they have specified. It shows you've listened to them and honored their request.

After the original follow-up, send a few more emails every two to four weeks, depending on the individual's circumstances.

It's more interesting and engaging to make each way of connecting a little different. In one email, send a testimonial from a client who has worked with you. In another email, summarize the benefits commonly experienced by your coaching clients. In another email, send a link to an article or blog post you think could be helpful.

Each of these follow-up messages demonstrate your desire to build a relationship. It also reflects your commitment to the individual; that builds trust and loyalty, thereby increasing the Know-Like-Trust factor.

While I do recommend that you personalize emails, it would be a proactive time saver for you to have some templates that can be easily tweaked to personalize the communication. This will save you time and energy.

Here is a seven-step follow-up sequence you can use:

	What to Do	When
1	During the Sample Session, ask how and when to follow up with them, and then create a calendar reminder.	
2	At the scheduled time, follow up just like they've requested (DM, email, text, phone).	
3	Send a handwritten note in the mail.	Two weeks later
4	Email with a testimonial from a client.	Two weeks later
5	Email that shows the benefits people commonly receive from coaching with you.	Three weeks later
6	Email with an article or blog post that would be a helpful resource.	Four weeks later

7	Email with a recommendation for a YouTube video or comment on a current news story that would be of interest to them.	Four weeks later

Action Checklist:

- ★ **Track your efforts.**

- ★ **Actively document contact attempts and methods.**

- ★ **Schedule for follow-up regularly.**

- ★ **Remember the rule of five contacts. Don't give up after just a couple of follow-ups.**

- ★ **Come from a place of service, kindness, and caring.**

- ★ **Specifically ask, "When and how shall I follow up with you?"**

- ★ **Respect the client's desired means of follow-up.**

- ★ **Believe in yourself.**

STRATEGY #3:
LEVERAGE REFERRALS

Using referrals is a great way to build your business right from the start. Leveraging referrals once your business is off the ground is another profitable way to keep your client roster filled.

Many professionals use referrals as a mainstay in their business. It's a great low-cost option that allows you to start a new relationship with a level of trust already established. Clients who come from referrals are more likely to sign on with you—an incredible 50% more likely—and much more likely to give their own referrals. It's a virtuous cycle.

When you use the referral method to grow your business, it's vitally important to have well-defined processes and deliver stellar service and results. Note, I didn't say flawless service, because after all, we're all human. Making mistakes and owning the responsibility with an open and transparent customer-focused mindset will also continue to build trust. But you must have strong integrity and be trustworthy to garner enough faith to get referrals from your clients.

This strategy can be broken down into two parts.

Part 1: Engage your friends, business network, and family to expand your coaching business when you are just starting out.

This is an effective way to build your client base quickly because the people you are asking already Know-Like-Trust you, which smooths the way and provides a warm introduction to you and your services.

How you do it:

Invite each of your family, friends, and peers to a Sample Session so they can understand what coaching is and can then see the advantages for themselves. When you are done, ask them: "Who do you know that would benefit from coaching?"

Bonus tip: If they themselves are also interested in coaching, you could refer them via your coaching collective (Strategy #10) or on a Facebook Group (Strategy # 5) to a peer.

Part 2: Ask your existing and past clients for referrals.

The best people to ask for recommendations are the ones who have experienced your work—the clients that you have coached for some time and who have received the direct value of how much you and your coaching have benefited their life.

Satisfied and engaged clients are generous with referrals (sometimes without even asking, which feels like such a gift). You turn those referrals into introductions, so the new prospect will be open to hearing from you. From that introduction, you set an appointment to hold a Sample

Session and add them to your regular newsletter email list. During your Sample Session, coach like crazy and make an impact; really help them to make progress, then you decide if you would like to work together. When you gain a new client, you provide even more value to them during your contract, and the cycle starts all over again.

It's simple. It's easy. And you can get started *right now.* You don't need any complicated preparations.

One of the beautiful aspects of this way to grow your coaching business is that it does not result in linear growth, i.e., one new client at a time. This process creates exponential growth, where one client can lead to two, two to four, four to eight, and so on. Your business grows exponentially in a way that is easy, organic, and enjoyable.

Ask your new, ongoing, and past clients for referrals at various touchpoints in your relationship.

For example:

1. During your Sample Sessions, be sure to tell the potential client that one of the most common ways you grow your business is by referral. This primes them to understand how you work and do a couple of other things as well. First, they are not surprised when you begin asking for referrals. Second, this explanation sets you apart, above many other coaches in your industry. Experts and trusted professionals get referrals, and you

have claimed your spot in that category. A referral is only given when the Know-Like-Trust factor is firmly in place. It's a way of establishing credibility without bragging about yourself.

At the end of your Sample Session ask them for a referral, regardless of whether they sign up for coaching or not.

2. Once a new client has started to get results and the relationship is more established, make sure to ask them for referrals too to keep developing your business.

3. Ask clients who are wrapping up their coaching contract during your completion session and when you send your feedback form, which you will use to gather testimonials and information on how you can better serve your clientele.

4. Keep in touch with past clients through personalized emails and ask them for referrals as part of your regular communication process.

You can also ask past clients if they would like to begin coaching again. Essentially, they refer themselves back to your coaching. People are busy, and you never know when they've been thinking of starting coaching again. Maybe they've been meaning to get in touch with you. These personalized emails make it so easy for them to hit reply and re-register.

You could even offer an incentive if you feel it's appropriate.

Some examples of referral incentives:

1. All people who refer a client to me this month are entered into a drawing for one free coaching session.

2. Or, all people who refer a client to me this month will receive a complimentary copy of my newly released book.

3. Or, all people who refer a client to me this month will receive a gift card for $25.

4. Or, all people who refer a client to me this month will receive a guest blog spot and honourable mention in my industry-leading newsletter. Use this approach when you are a business coach. This way you help your clients' businesses to succeed too by giving them free visibility.

How to do it:

You can't just ask for a referral once and never mention it again. You need to ask repeatedly, but you also need to be discerning. Asking for referrals is important, but you don't want to bombard your clients with this request.

One suggestion is to schedule it in your Customer Relationship Management tool (CRM). Your CRM can be an integrated app, an Excel spreadsheet, a paper journal, or in the "notes" section of your mobile phone.

All you need to do is send a genuinely friendly and personal note to each of your clients from time to time. Once every three months is a reasonable frequency for follow-up. In this note, you will connect, touch base, and perhaps even provide a helpful resource. And, as part of the note, you can ask for referrals.

You could say something like this:

> *Dear Jane,*
>
> *I was thinking about you the other day and your new job. I'd love to hear how it is going for you, and I wish you every success. I found this article online that made me think of you. I hope you enjoy it and find it useful: https://xxxx.com.*
>
> *I have some openings in my schedule for new clients, and since I enjoyed working with you, I thought I would ask who you might know that would benefit from coaching.*
>
> *Thanks, and I look forward to hearing from you soon.*

The key here is to use the phrase "who do you know" as opposed to "do you know anyone." The first phrase prompts their brain to automatically search for a solution to this problem and is more likely to produce a referral than the second phrase which has an easy "yes" or "no" answer. Since we're wired to solve problems and answer questions, once they've responded "yes" or "no," their natural brain activity will feel that this problem is solved so they will no longer focus on solving the question/problem. It's a natural brain activity, so you might as well leverage it.

You also should periodically ask your clients, either at the end of a session or during a regular touchpoint call. Once every five or six conversations is a good interval. You don't want to bombard your clients, but you want them to remember referrals are important to you.

For each referral you receive, send a genuine heartfelt thank you note via snail mail, or pick up the phone and call the person who made the recommendation. You want to honour and reward that they thought highly enough of you and your service that they wanted to share it with another. You are thanking them for the act of referring and for the trust they have shown. Be generous with your gratitude. Do not hinge your gratitude on whether the person starts coaching with you or not.

Once you have a referral, reach out to the new person who's been referred to you, and invite them to experience a no-pressure Sample Session.

Finally, add this text to your email signature and your appointment confirmation template to keep it top of mind:

Many of my clients come through referrals. If you know someone who would benefit from coaching, please send them my way for a free, no-obligation Sample Session.

STRATEGY #4:
LAUNCH WITH A BANG!

The purpose of launching a business, product, or service is to create a buzz and generate clients.

Imagine a rocket launching. There is fanfare, a countdown, and the drama of anticipation. A flurry of excitement is in the air, and everyone knows about it!

With some strategic planning you will be able to fan the flames and generate a massive influx of new clients to your business.

Let's explore how!

Grab your calendar and determine when you want to launch your practice.

You must plan the necessary and exact steps well in advance. Giving yourself a good two to three weeks preparation time, and stick with it! Then make sure you have ample time blocked off on your calendar to deliver all the coaching sessions booked with the launch. Set up your scheduler with your available time slots so you don't find yourself scrambling to find time in your calendar.

Ask yourself the following:

"How long do I want my launch to be?"

For example, will it last for three days, or will you stretch it out across one week?

"How will I be announcing my big launch?"

I recommend telling everyone you know by email, in person, and on social media! Ask your friends and peers to share the announcements with their networks too!

Plan your social media blitz and create a launch calendar. Create a special launch folder on your computer so everything is easily organized and in one place. Write the announcements and create the necessary graphics so everything is ready to go.

Write the emails and schedule them in your email service provider. Prepare a minimum of three emails: the initial announcement, a reminder email, and a final email announcing that your offer is soon expiring.

Continue asking yourself:

"What special promotional offer will I be promoting?"

Will it be a significant discount, or, buy one get one free? And will it be a one-time special?

Be very clear about terms and conditions.

For example, if you are offering a discounted rate for thirty days, what will the charge be after those thirty days?

Or if it's a one-time special, how many sessions will they get at that rate, and what date must the sessions be completed by?

Another possible example: "You will get a 75% discount on my silver coaching package, but you must register and pay in full no later than May 15th."

Keep your timelines tight to create a sense of urgency and give people fair warning. You can say, "If you don't act by this date, you won't be able to access this awesome deal!"

Clearly state your expectation in response to the promotional deal, e.g.: "In exchange for this 90% discount, I would love it if you would give me a testimonial I can use as I grow my business."

Remember to explain what coaching entails, the results they will experience, and make it very clear how to sign up.

Determine ahead of time what you will post and how often. You will need to share the announcements multiple times across your various social media networks. Commit to posting twice a day, every day, for one week to build momentum.

Video creates awesome anticipation for launches! Record a video and embed it in your emails.

Utilize Facebook Live and Instagram Stories, so your excitement can be seen and heard, not just read.

Action Checklist:

- 📌 **Determine your launch date.**

- 📌 **Create a launch calendar giving yourself at least three weeks lead time.**

- 📌 **Create a specific launch folder on your computer.**

- 📌 **Get crystal clear on your special offers or promotions.**

- 📌 **Be very specific about your expectations, terms, and conditions.**

- 📌 **Write all announcements and place in the launch folder.**

- 📌 **Prepare necessary graphics and put in launch folder.**

- 📌 **Set up your scheduler to accommodate launch-generated appointments.**

- 📌 **Draft three announcement emails: announcement, reminder, and last call!**

- 📌 **Schedule the three launch messages with your email service provider.**

- ★ **Schedule your media blitz.**
- ★ **Ask every one of your contacts to please share the messages.**
- ★ **Embrace video!**
- ★ **Incorporate video in all your emails and social media posts!**
- ★ **Track all efforts.**
- ★ **Schedule all efforts for regular follow-up.**
- ★ **Respect your timeline.**

STRATEGY #5:
FACEBOOK AND SOCIAL MEDIA

While in-person networking is important, online networking can expand your reach beyond geographical borders. Since coaching is rapidly exploding via telephone and video conferencing, it makes sense to broaden your networking efforts. Let's turn an eye toward the online world, specifically: social media.

Social media is always evolving—new platforms are being added and different groups flock to their favorite platform. This means you'll need to identify which social media platform is the most popular with your preferred client base.

Facebook has countless groups! These are an excellent way to meet new people and share information, videos, or photos. They can also be used to make plans and deliver inspirational and educational content.

Keep in mind if you are not a Facebook user or your ideal clients congregate on another platform such as LinkedIn, Snapchat, or Instagram, the approach will be similar. The only difference is the terminology and variability between social media platforms.

GROUPS TO WHICH YOUR IDEAL CLIENTS BELONG

Just as your ideal client hangs out in certain places in real life, they do the same thing on social media.

Begin by allocating a couple of hours to research potential Facebook groups. Keep in mind the following questions while researching:

» Do the members fit your ideal client profile?

» Is the group large or small? How many members are there?

» Is it a group simply for sharing, or do they have active discussions?

» How many conversations are ongoing?

» Is the tone of the group supportive, or is it primarily a place to complain?

» Are there any red flags or things that concern you when you're reviewing the feed?

» What topic is the group centered around?

» Do you have to join a paid program to be part of the group?

» Do you have to live in a specific community?

» Are there any other prerequisites for being a member?

» What are the group guidelines?

I do not recommend you join every possible group. This is a strategy that will require continuity and genuine effort. It is best to select the top three to five highly engaged groups that align well with your ideal client and the issues you hope to support them in.

Read the community guidelines thoroughly and ask to join.

Once you have been accepted, post a "thank you" to the administrators for adding you.

Many groups ask for a brief introduction with a short bio and photo. Draft a bio that is friendly, clear, and helpful. Briefly touch on your coaching business, not as a sales pitch, but as an authentic explanation of who you are.

It is always good to include a flattering photograph of yourself. In this case, your professional headshot may not be the right choice. Choose a photo that aligns with the group's tone and dynamic. For example, if you have joined a group for spiritual healers or stay-at-home-parents, don't use a headshot of you wearing ultra-conservative business attire.

Becoming an active participant in these groups is another component of great networking. It spreads the word of your business, who you are, what you do, and how you support your clients.

These groups are about give and take: conversation, collaboration, and connection.

Many groups have guidelines in place to prevent spamming. Your online reputation is just as important as how you behave in person. It is difficult to regain respect once it has been lost.

Set a specific schedule you will adhere to while utilizing social media. You could review the notifications everyday, and then comment on any relevant questions or discussions where you can support a fellow member or add value to the discussion.

It's better to frequent the group less often, but to be consistent.

For example, don't be in there three times a day for the first two days and then not contribute at all for the rest of the month. If all you can do is once a day, do it every day for the week. When you show up consistently, people will begin recognizing your name and profile photo. You will begin creating a personal connection with them.

Write helpful, thoughtful responses to members' questions. This increases your visibility, and you become recognizable as a helpful member while building your authority.

If the administrators ask for assistance, be the one that steps forward and volunteers. It can be tough running a community, and being of assistance helps the community grow. It is a win-win for all of you.

Be a regular participant in the group for at least three to six months. You probably won't get any results the first few weeks, and it can be easy to give up when you don't see a fast payoff. But if you stick with it, you will have people become naturally curious about your business, begin to follow your own social media posts, and even ask for your assistance and/or feedback.

If during your Facebook group research, you realize there is a gap in the market for your ideal client, then go ahead and create your own to fill that need!

CREATING YOUR OWN FACEBOOK GROUP

A few considerations when creating a new group:

» When deciding on a name, you will want it to clearly convey the purpose of the group. If you can, make it appealing and fun.

» Create your community guidelines. Use another community's rules for a frame of reference, then customize your own group's guidelines.

» The Facebook "help" feature is a great source of information. Select "help" and search "How do I start a group?" Since social media platforms are constantly being tweaked, the "help" feature is the best way to stay up-to-date on developments.

You may find it helpful to have these instructions open on your mobile phone, or print them, so they can be close at hand while you complete the setup on your computer or laptop.

Once you have the group set up, send invitations to people who fit your group criteria. You may have the ability to add people of your choice, but don't do it! Be aware that if you add people to your group without their permission, it will backfire. People like to be in control of what they view, and how they participate on social media.

Creating your own group will require you to allocate more time to establish the desired tone and to ensure all members abide by your guidelines.

Overall, creating your own Facebook group is an excellent way to leapfrog to the front of the line and establish your online authority. So, if you are eager to make some fast headway, dive in and use this strategy!

COACH NETWORKS ON FACEBOOK

In-person networking is important, but online networking can expand your reach to areas you wouldn't usually be able to reach—other cities, provinces, states, and countries. Since coaching is a rapidly expanding industry in which you can provide service to anyone with a telephone or internet, it is a good idea to broaden the geography of your networking also.

There is great potential in Facebook groups! Specifically, there are Facebook networking groups for coaches.

To make practical use of this online strategy it is imperative you are abundantly clear on your specialty. "Life coach" is not a specialty. "Life coach who helps mid-career professionals achieve more of a work-life balance," for example, is a speciality.

Once again, your Signature Sentence will be brought into action!

Keep in mind that every word you type on social media and every group you join is public information. The quality of your online reputation is important: guard it carefully and always act with integrity.

It is best to begin with only one coaching networking Facebook group so you can invest your time and energy wisely. As with many of the other strategies described, consistency will be key.

These coaching networking groups will have strict guidelines, and it is important you respect them as such.

Introduce yourself. Be helpful and respectful and become an integral part of the group. These groups are based on give-and-take collaboration. Support your fellow members; don't join solely for your own gain.

In these groups you may learn a helpful tip or have a great conversation. They are great for asking specific questions and receiving feedback. Write helpful, thoughtful responses to members' questions, but only respond to requests where your expertise matches what has been asked for. Stick with your strengths in these coaching groups. Trying to get clients outside of your zone of expertise will hamper your long-term success.

Supporting your peers expands your skillset and demonstrates you are a helpful resource and an important part of the coaching community. When you are careful about how you respond and to what you respond, you are showing people your integrity. It quickly becomes evident who is valuable and who is helpful and committed, as well as who is a flake and/or only there for their own gain.

Schedule time in your calendar to check in on the group activity regularly.

Often there are referral posts where people are looking to find a coach. Respond to these calls both for yourself, as well as recommending other coaches you know could be a good fit. When responding to these posts, respect the person's wishes. If they ask for a private message or email, respond as such. Don't put your contact details in the thread. When you disregard their instructions, you've started the relationship off on a potentially tenuous footing, and more than likely, you won't be looked on favorably.

Online life coaching network groups can be a valuable resource. You may meet a potential client in real life who isn't a fit for your services, but one of the other group members may be a perfect match.

Remember... a rising tide lifts all ships! Coaching is still a relatively new profession. By promoting it and helping build the coaching industry as a collective whole, all good coaches will benefit!

Action Checklist:

- 📌 **Have your Signature Sentence prepared.**

- 📌 **Be crystal clear on your coaching specialty.**

- 📌 **Research a variety of Facebook groups—where your ideal client hangs out, as well as coach networking groups.**

- 📌 **Request to join the top two.**

- 📌 **When your membership is approved, respect all group guidelines.**

- 📌 **Introduce yourself, offer thanks for being added to the group, and respond respectfully with care and consideration.**

- 📌 **Create a schedule to maintain your presence in the group.**

- 📌 **Be consistent.**

- 📌 **Don't spam.**

- 📌 **Adhere to your social media schedule.**

STRATEGY #6:
GET FACE-TO-FACE

The easiest, most efficient way to attract clients is to spend time where your potential customers are. You must get out amongst your customers, so you can demonstrate how you can change their life according to your specialty.

Coaching is still a relatively new profession, and many people don't know what it is. It is important to both tell them and show them, thereby educating people about your services. The more they understand the benefit, the more inclined they will be to seek it.

Establish relationships and invite people to experience a Sample Session.

Where do you think your ideal clients gather?

Set your timer and do a quick brainstorm of all the places they may gather... classes, conferences, social events, training sessions, gyms, studios, shops, libraries, and cafes! ... yoga classes, walking groups, book clubs, wine tastings, waiting on the sidelines at their children's recreational events ... the possibilities are almost endless!

Go old school—put your phone away and get out from behind your computer. Keep an eye out for local events you can attend and meet new people. Attend these in-person events.

Visit places where your ideal client would hang out, and meet new people face-to-face!

MEET SOMEONE NEW!

Getting out and meeting people is a strategy that will require an invested commitment. Don't attend an event one time and never go back. It is better to attend one or two activities a month than to visit ten separate events once and never return.

We all have our own comfort levels, and it is important to select events where you will be able to enjoy yourself. When you feel happy and excited, you will be more comfortable meeting new people and introducing yourself.

Grab your calendar and commit to yourself how often you'd like to go out. Again, keep in mind you need to choose to participate for an extended period. This is not a "one and done" approach. You want to weave yourself within the fabric of a group, and that takes time.

Initially you may only speak with one person, but over time, you will get more and more opportunities to participate and meet new people.

Let's face it—"What do you do?" is one of the top three small talk questions! What an amazing opportunity to use your Signature Sentence.

Remember, your goal is not to "sell." Your goal is to create genuine connections and establish new relationships, to build and expand on the "Know-Like-Trust" factor.

Over time, you are going to get so many opportunities to talk about what you do! When people express an interest, this is the natural opportunity to invite them to a Sample Session!

Action Checklist:

- ✒ **Commit to getting out and meeting new people.**

- ✒ **Do a quick brainstorm of where your ideal client is likely to hang out.**

- ✒ **Create a goal of how many times per week you will do such.**

- ✒ **Commit on your calendar.**

- ✒ **Regularly update your contact list with names and contact information.**

- ✒ **Track your efforts.**

- ✒ **Schedule for regular and appropriate follow-up.**

STRATEGY #7:
VOLUNTEER

When you volunteer, not only will you improve your coaching skills, you will also have the opportunity to expand your network and grow your contact list. Plus, you can gather some terrific testimonials that can be leveraged to grow your practice.

In addition, many organizations offer honorariums to participating coaches. It may not be a lot of money, but being paid to grow your skills and level of experience can be a great opportunity.

Volunteering is a great way to share your skills with those who otherwise may not have access to quality coaching. Reaching people outside the range of your usual network is an added benefit!

Organizations that support individuals to rise beyond their current situation are most likely in need of coaches. These are an excellent place to begin your search for volunteer opportunities.

To find potential volunteer opportunities:

» Do a Google search using common terms such as: "volunteer life coaching opportunities," "volunteer opportunities near me," or "where can I volunteer as a life coach?"

» Review the websites of organizations that strike a chord with you, asking yourself:

  1. Do I resonate with their mission?

  2. Do the people portrayed on the website excite me?

  3. What criteria do they have for volunteers?

  4. Do I meet their criteria?

  5. What time commitment is necessary?

  6. Do I need to travel to their site, or can I coach from my home?

There is usually a "contact us" link, or you can search right on the site for the volunteer coordinator.

Send a note or email to ask when they do volunteer intake and find out more about volunteering.

Altruism and charity work is rewarding for everyone involved. It can be a great way to re-energize yourself and feel the benefits of helping others in need.

Action Checklist:

- ★ Are you interested in volunteering?

- ★ Clarify what demographic with which you would like to volunteer.

- ★ What time commitment can you make?

- ★ Research volunteer opportunities in your area.

- ★ Approach accordingly.

- ★ Track your efforts.

- ★ Schedule for appropriate follow-up.

STRATEGY #8:
CRAIGSLIST

Once you have exhausted your immediate circle and contact list, Craigslist is an oddly effective place to connect, whether looking for Sample Sessions, to recruit your first few clients, or to supplement existing coaching income!

Admittedly, Craigslist is not the source of top-paying clients. But the method works well to provide a steady stream of clients. Before you reject the idea of lower-paying clients, let's explore the long-term value of a client for a moment.

Let's say you charge $100 an hour for a coaching session and you coach the average client for twelve sessions. One Craigslist client can be worth $1,200. Plus, if that one person gives you referrals, they are worth even more to your business! Say three referrals at $100 per session x 12 sessions = $3600!

Begin with some quick research... are there any other coaches on Craigslist in your area?

Open a fresh Word document on your computer or use a note on your mobile phone to draft the details of your ad so you can easily cut and paste it onto the Craigslist website.

Include in your draft your rates, an enticing description, and a brief blurb about your coaching practice.

Remember you are highlighting the desired experience of your ideal customer. Focus on how your coaching expertise will serve your client! Be very specific regarding logistics: price, frequency, who you are looking to work with and how you will conduct the coaching (i.e. on the phone or video conference).

Here are two examples of possible Craigslist advertisements:

<u>Example #1:</u>

I am a certified coach working towards accreditation with the International Coaching Federation. To accumulate hours, I am offering a limited time discounted rate of $30 per one-hour session! If you are interested in working with a coach to achieve your health or career goals, I look forward to hearing from you.

<u>Example #2:</u>

Do you want to up level your business to the potential heights you have dreamt of? Are you eager to explore ideas to implement carefully-honed strategies to ensure success? An honest, straightforward business-educated entrepreneur is here to help you! Together we will explore your goals and identify specific steps necessary to increase revenue!

You can always choose to include more information about yourself in the description. For example:

About Me and My Coaching Approach

My coaching style is one of collaborative partnership ... My intention is to provide thought-provoking questions to unearth the discovery of your own answers. It is an honour to support individuals in pursuit of their goals, to witness their dreams become reality and living their best life!

I am qualified to support you in the following arenas:

» Prioritizing your health and well-being

» Achieving work / life balance

» Providing space to contemplate your own growth

» Exploring goals aligned with your core values

» Creating accountability in the pursuit of your authentic goals

» Identifying your strengths and exploring how they can help you move forward

» Creating joy and success in your life!

Utilizing the mind mapping and brainstorming completed in the Clarity and Preparation segments, use your research to craft an engaging headline. For your inspiration, here are some examples:

» Looking for a Life Coach? $50 Per Session.

» One-Hour Complimentary Business Coaching Session.

» Career Reinvention Coach Helps You Find the Job You Love!

» Achieve Your Ideal Body Weight with Transformation Coaching!

» Dating Coach Reveals How the Top 1% of Women Have Men Chasing Them!

Utilize spellcheck and verify grammar before uploading your draft. Read the piece aloud to ensure it is fluid and makes sense. You are presenting yourself as a professional; overlooking these details will be detrimental.

You are now ready to upload your draft to the Craigslist website!

Start by selecting your area on the upper, righthand side of the Craigslist screen. Place your cursor on the field and enter the name of the city closest to you. It will automatically pull up a city for you to confirm your location.

Under the question "What type of posting is this?" select "Service offered." Then specify the category of service provided. Coaching can be promoted under either "small biz ads" or "therapeutic services."

Copy your attention-grabbing headline from your carefully proofread and saved draft, and paste it directly into the correct fields.

To make the headline stand out, use some appropriately placed all caps. But remember to use discretion; too many capitalized letters and it will appear you are yelling. NO ONE WANTS TO WORK WITH A YELLING COACH!

Here are three examples for you to consider the effect of using capitalized titles:

1. Achieve Your Ideal Body Weight with Transformational Coaching!

2. Achieve Your IDEAL BODY WEIGHT with Transformational Coaching!

3. ACHIEVE YOUR IDEAL BODY WEIGHT WITH TRANSFORMATIONAL COACHING!!

Enter your service description next.

Be sure to include a disclaimer in your ad clearly stating that coaching is not therapy nor is it a substitute for counselling. One disclaimer sample for your consideration:

"Coaching is not a substitute for legal, medical, psychological, financial, business, or other such professional counsel."

Select whether you are licensed with the appropriate checkbox.

You will be prompted to specify how clients are to contact you; I recommend you use the Craigslist email relay option. This keeps your personal information safe and secure.

You will be asked if you want your location to show up on a map. I strongly recommend against this, as your address is most likely your home.

Lastly, you will be asked to specify if it is okay for others to contact you about services, products, or other commercial interests. Select "Do not contact me with unsolicited services or offers."

Once all the information has been entered, I encourage you to upload a photo that represents your business. Photographs make it more likely for someone to reply to your ad.

Finally, you will be presented with a preview of your unpublished draft. Review it *carefully* and make any necessary adjustments before clicking "Publish."

The advertisement will not be published until you pay the fee, and it will expire in thirty days. I recommend refreshing your post every few days to push it back up to the top.

A NOTE REGARDING PERSONAL SAFETY

The overwhelming majority of Craigslist users are trustworthy with good intentions, but of course, there are exceptions.

Do not give out your telephone number, email address, or other personal contact information. Instead use the Craigslist supplied email address with the comment "Please email me with any questions you may have."

There is no reason for you to meet in person.

Instead, elect to coach by video conference instead of sharing your phone number, personal details, or planning to actually meet in person. Some people have poor boundaries, and so it is best to take these reasonable precautions.

Action Checklist:

- ★ **Clarify your objective: are you advertising your services or inviting Sample Sessions?**

- ★ **Investigate if there are any other coaches advertising in your area.**

- ★ **Draft your advertisement.**

- ★ **Utilize your mind mapping to brainstorm information from the Clarity Segment.**

* Proofread your advertisement.

* What graphics will you include?

* Create your Craigslist account.

* Post your advertisement.

* Pay advertisement fee.

* Track your advertisement date.

* Schedule to refresh posting as necessary.

STRATEGY #9:
CREATE A BUSINESS REFERRAL NETWORK

Business referral networks are collaborative groups of business owners that refer clients to one another. This method of collaboration is a natural fit with coaching practices. These are reciprocal relationships in which the leads and referrals go both ways.

Business referral networks are win-win arrangements!

Begin by considering your ideal client: what needs do they have that you are not equipped to provide?

For example, a family and parenting coaching client may require child care, tutoring, nutritional and meal planning, legal services, home mortgage / banking / financial services, family fun activities, consignment stores ... so on and so forth!

Another example, many business owners who are being coached need services such as bookkeeping, legal services, website design and development, virtual assistants, marketing services, social media support, etc.

When you are clear on your coaching niche, set a timer and brainstorm a list of services your ideal clients regularly use.

Ask yourself: "What types of service providers do my clients need?" and "How many referrals do I want?"

Who do you know that you could recommend to your clients?

Keep in mind that since this is a referral, your reputation will be affected by the quality of service provided by whomever you refer. Make sure you are 100% confident with those to whom you reach out.

Initially your list of potential referrals may be small, but you will be filling in missing services over time.

Prepare a high-level partnership plan for your business referral network. Be crystal clear of the benefits of this collaboration and *communicate your expectations clearly* when introducing the concept to other small business owners.

Will you be asking for a simple introduction to potential clients, or, will you be asking for a recommendation plus an introductory email so you can follow up on potential leads?

When you are crystal clear on what you desire from a business referral network, you can begin reaching out to potential collaborators one at a time and request a meeting.

Present your partnership plan and establish ground rules during your initial discussions.

After your initial meeting, you have a responsibility to decide if you think this person will be an upstanding member of your business referral network. Do you think they will benefit you, enhance your reputation, and support your clients well?

After your initial meeting, always send a follow-up note thanking them for their time. If your initial meeting goes well, set up a second meeting to have a more in-depth discussion in which details can be finalized before including them in your referral network.

If you notice any red flags or are uncomfortable in any way, *respect your intuition!* Send them a simple note thanking them for their interest, but advising you have found another option that better meets your clients' needs.

Finalize any verbal agreement with a letter confirming your arrangement, and send a copy to your new referral partner.

As you get to know your coaching clients better, continue adding to your list of services and continue seeking experts your clients will regularly need and use.

Keep your master Referral Network up to date, and continue touching base regularly with your referral partners so you stay in the forefront of their minds. You want it to be a win-win. It may feel unbalanced in the short term; however, focus on the long-term benefit to you, your referral partners, and your clients.

BUSINESS REFERRAL NETWORK

Service	Company	Contact Person	Email	Phone
Before and after school day care	ABC Daycare	Sandra Play	ABCD@ gmail.com	123-456-7890
Mortgage / Banking	XYZ Bank	Laurie Aames	lauriea@ xyzbank. com	404-555-1234
Family fun activities				
Travel	123 Travel	John Brown	familyfun@ travel.com	231-987-5089
Consignment store				
Nutrition and meal planning				
Personal training				
Sleep and self care experts				
Legal services	Dice & Associates	Rick Dice	rdice@ dicelaw.com	205-555-9876

Client Referred Date of Referral		Feedback
Sally Jones	Feb 23/18	My kids are so happy going there!
West Johnson	June 4/18	Very professional, easy to work with
Sam Smith	July 29/18	Best trip ever
Karen Nelson	March 17/18	Reasonable rates, honest, prompt

Action Checklist:

- ★ **Brainstorm potential service providers your client base will utilize.**

- ★ **Establish a plan and ground rules for participants in your referral network.**

- ★ **Research potential business partners.**

- ★ **Set up an initial meeting.**

- ★ **Send a "thank you" for their time.**

- ★ **Schedule a follow-up meeting if proceeding.**

- ★ **Finalize details and submit to partners.**

- ★ **Keep your master Referral Network list up-to-date.**

- ★ **Touch base with the network partners regularly.**

- ★ **Track your efforts.**

- ★ **Schedule for follow-up as necessary.**

STRATEGY #10:
INITIATE A COACHING COLLECTIVE

There is an African proverb: "If you want to go fast, go alone. If you want to go far, go together."

A coaching collective is a referral exchange network with like-minded coaches collaborating to expand each member's client base and supporting one another along the journey.

Family and friends don't always support us in the way that is the most helpful. Often they don't understand what coaching is; they may think coaching is woo-woo and be suspicious about it. They naturally worry about us.

When I began my own coaching practice, so often one of my relatives would say, "You've got a great job with benefits. How could you not be satisfied with that? Do your time and you'll retire well off! Why would you risk that?"

Not everyone will understand your desire to build a business. They may mean well, but you have probably found out that many of your friends and family don't understand what you are trying to achieve.

It is common to have a tough time and feel discouraged from time to time. A coaching collective is an excellent support network for everyone involved, minimizing discouragement and downtime. True support from your peers will help you immeasurably!

Begin by deciding if you will take the initiative to spearhead the creation of a group yourself, or if you wish to find a coaching friend to help facilitate. Creating a coaching collective will take some work, time, and energy, but it costs nothing.

Things to consider when initiating a coaching collective:

» Are you initiating this independently, or will you have a co-chair?

» What will the collective's mission be?

» What will the ground rules be?

» How many members will there be?

» What levels of coaches will you include?

» How often will the collective be meeting?

» How will you recruit potential members?

It is important the coaching collective be a manageable size. I recommend six to eight members. If a collective is too small, there isn't enough leverage and there won't be enough referrals to make it useful. If it is too large, it will be hard to create connection between the members, and it will be difficult to maintain.

Before inviting other coaches to participate, it is good to establish the group's mission, ground rules, and guiding principles. Are you establishing the group to encourage one another when establishing practices, or are you looking to refer potential clients to one another?

GROUND RULES AND MISSION

Ask yourself the following:

» Will you expect each member to attend meetings?

» How are they expected to participate?

» Will you have a minimum quota regarding monthly referrals to other members?

» Will members be asked to leave if they aren't providing referrals?

» What commitment do you expect from each member?

» How long do you want the coaching collective to continue?

» How often will the collective meet?

When the ground rules, guiding principles, and group mission have been established, you can begin researching and inviting potential members. These may be people you've met through your own training or through networking measures.

POTENTIAL MEMBERS

What level of coaches will you be including in this collective? Will it be only new coaches starting out, or a mix of newbies and established practitioners? Will it only be open to coaches trained in the same methodology?

You want to make sure each member of the group is crystal clear on their coaching niche. This keeps coming up as a common theme in this book because I cannot emphasize the power that comes from clarity!

As the initiator of the collective, it is important you don't look for members that will conflict with your expertise. You are looking for a good mix of members who complement one another rather than compete with one another. For example, you don't want two executive coaches focused on C-Suite female leaders.

The following are two examples of coaching collective memberships for your consideration.

Example #1:

A self-care specialist, an executive coach, a career coach, a nutrition and exercise authority, a parenting coach, and finally a relationship coach.

Example #2:

A coach specializing in retirement transition, one who focuses exclusively on supporting newly separated/divorced people, a weight loss coach, a career consultant, a business coach specializing in start-ups, and a life coach that supports creatives discovering and living their life purpose.

INITIATING

When the group is initially formed, it is important to initiate with some icebreaker meetings. Perhaps each member takes the floor to introduce themselves, explain what they're looking for, and describe how the group can support them best. This is also excellent ground for each of you to practice your elevator pitches and Signature Sentences.

When a group of committed coaches come together with the intention of creating long-term success for all members, each will benefit more than you could on your own.

MEETING

Meet regularly to allow each member's connection to deepen. Track the referral activity so members know where they stand, and to ensure each are equally contributing and receiving value from the process.

Action Checklist:

📌 **Decide if you will be initiating a collective on your own or with a co-facilitator.**

📌 **Decide on the collective's mission.**

📌 **Establish ground rules.**

📌 **Clarify the ideal number of members.**

📌 **Determine what level of coaches will be included.**

📌 **Clarify the level of participating and commitment expected from members.**

📌 **Decide how meetings will be facilitated.**

📌 **Decide how often meetings will be held.**

📌 **Ensure no overlap with participants' specialties.**

📌 **Recruit potential members.**

📌 **Track your efforts.**

📌 **Schedule for follow up.**

📌 **Initiate first meeting.**

STRATEGY #11:
DEAL SITES

People are always looking to save money, and there is a plethora of deal sites worldwide. In my region, Groupon is currently the most popular. Every day, individuals scroll through the deal sites looking for exciting things to do and solutions to their problems. The beauty of this strategy is being advertised on their website and promoted with their massive email client lists!

While deal sites take a sizable percentage of each sale, the advertising you receive alone is well worth it! Further, once the promotion is set up, you don't need to do anything more than welcome new clients as they approach you. Many of the clients I have worked with through deal sites continue to use my coaching services regularly, and they are clients I would never have met any other way.

This is a very low effort way of getting your first clients or fill in some blank appointments in your schedule.

Details for each deal site vary, and you will have to be flexible. They have strict guidelines regarding promotions, e.g., they generally will not allow two coaches in the same geographic region offering the same coaching packages. They also have mandates regarding photographs and content.

To utilize a deal site, you must have a website. It doesn't have to be complicated, but it does need to be professional and attractive. I also recommend you have an email address that reflects your domain name.

Decide on your objective in advance before posting your offer.

Ask yourself, "Do I want to use the deal site as a way of facilitating more Sample Sessions?"

or

"Do I want to use the deal site as a method of selling low-cost coaching packages?".

If you are using this platform to generate more Sample Sessions, you will want your deal to be for a single session as an opportunity to offer a higher-priced coaching package. This is a great way to polish delivering professional Sample Sessions and practice making your pitch to prospective clients. Plus, as your skill level improves you will recruit clients in your higher-priced coaching packages.

If you are using the deal site to sell low-cost coaching packages, I recommend multi-session packages of four to six sessions.

Too few sessions will fail to provide the client with results.

Too many sessions will frustrate you with diminished revenue for your efforts.

I recommend setting your rates reasonably when utilizing the deal site strategy. If your prices are too low, the service you provide is undervalued, and you will feel frustrated with the lack of compensation.

When you are clear on your desired experience, reach out to speak with a representative. They are accommodating and should patiently answer any of your questions and provide guidance regarding your promotion. Once you've decided how many new customers you are looking for, your assigned representative will ensure your offer meets your goals without exceeding your maximum capacity.

You will be asked to confirm your terms and conditions. For example, can someone buy the promoted deal more than once? Or can they buy it as a gift? You'll also be asked how long the offer will run for.

Be sure to read the terms and conditions carefully so you are informed. If there is anything you aren't clear on, or if you have any questions whatsoever, reach out to your account representative before signing the contract.

Once your promotional campaign is approved, it will take anywhere from twenty-four to seventy-two hours for the offer to become active. Then, when someone buys your promotion, they will email you with a voucher number. Be sure to respond to these new clients promptly, and double-check that their voucher is valid before providing your services.

Provide the same exemplary coaching experience to these clients as you would anyone else!

Be sure to encourage each person coached to leave you a top five-star review and offer a glowing testimonial. Good reviews will definitely encourage future potential customers.

Action Checklist:

- 📌 **Become very clear on your objective.**

- 📌 **Have your website ready.**

- 📌 **Research applicable deal sites.**

- 📌 **Determine your package and pricing.**

- 📌 **Approach deal site representative.**

- 📌 **Receive guidance from representative and remain flexible.**

- 📌 **Confirm terms and conditions of your offer.**

- 📌 **Have your promotional campaign approved by the deal site.**

📌 **Have your online scheduler ready with available spaces.**

145

📌 **Regularly update your master contacts list.**

📌 **Track your messages and replies.**

📌 **Schedule for regular follow-up.**

STRATEGY #12:
HOST A WORKSHOP

When you facilitate an in-person workshop, you immediately establish yourself as a credible expert!

Host a workshop and show potential clients how you will support them. This is a wonderful interactive way for people to experience coaching before committing to a full program. This is an amazingly effective way to get your business off the ground quickly and effectively!

I know this can sound like a scary proposition. Don't let your inner critic talk you out of this.

Let's explore the possibilities!

How you design and deliver your workshop is entirely up to you. It certainly doesn't have to be a full-day, catered event in a rented conference room. It can just as easily be a ninety-minute workshop in your living room, your local library, or a restaurant meeting room.

Think about it—if you host a workshop with twenty people and five of them sign on as clients, you could essentially fill your practice with just one or two workshops!

With a little bit of planning, strategy, and effort, a workshop is an amazingly worthwhile endeavour that I highly recommend.

The first time you do it, you want to make it as simple as possible while still providing excellent value to potential clients.

DECIDE ON THE TOPIC

Your goal is to demonstrate the power of coaching, connect with potential clients, and give the attendees practical information they can immediately implement to solve one specific issue.

The importance of a topic with easy steps and a tangible result can't be emphasized enough!

DECIDE ON LOCATION

Here are some affordable suggestions:

» Your living room

» Your back deck

» The local library

» Community centre

» A local restaurant or coffee shop with private meeting room

» Ask a friend or relative to borrow their lunch room/ meeting room at their office

» Rent a meeting room from a local business

» Rent a meeting room from a co-working space

SELECT THE DATE AND TIME

For your first workshop, keep it simple and short; plan on a ninety-minute time slot. Here's how to use the time for the greatest advantage...

Allow fifteen minutes for guests to arrive and get settled. Plan a sixty-minute long presentation. Assign fifteen minutes at the end for those in attendance to ask any questions, chat, and gather their things to leave.

The ideal time for your workshop depends on your target audience. If they are stay-at-home parents, you could offer the workshop in the afternoon before they pick their children up from school. If they commute downtown everyday, consider offering the workshop on a weeknight or a Saturday.

CREATE A GUEST LIST

The size of the space will determine the size of your guest list. If you are holding it in your living room and you have room for six to sit comfortably, that's the number of attendees.

I recommend inviting the number of people you would like to host and ask each of them to bring a guest. Not everyone will be able to attend, but if they bring a guest you have expanded the reach of potential clients and at the same time created a cushion to ensure you have the desired number of people attending.

EXTEND INVITATIONS

Your invitation approach is important!

Ask people to R.S.V.P. / confirm they will be attending.

Note I didn't say ask them *if* they will attend. *Assume* they will be attending, and ask for the confirmation. In addition, ask them who they will be bringing as a guest instead of asking *if* they are bringing someone. These two small tweaks immediately increase the number of people that will attend.

Send email invitations and follow up with telephone calls.

Your passion and enthusiasm are engaging. Be sure to express how excited you are to be delivering this workshop, and how much you are looking forward to seeing them!

PREPARING YOUR PRESENTATION

Creating a presentation that will introduce your coaching platform is not as difficult as you may think! The key is to make it an interactive experience, and brainstorm a variety of different ways to engage your attendees, such as: facilitate group discussion, provide a workbook, or offer a coaching demonstration.

"How will I fill the time?" you may be asking yourself. Here's a simple one hour-long workshop structure:

- → Five minutes to introduce yourself.

- → Twenty minutes to cover the featured subject.

- → Fifteen minutes to incorporate a brief coaching demonstration.

- → Five minutes to debrief the short coaching experience.

- → Ten minutes for questions.

- → Five minutes to wrap up and thank your guests for attending

To engage audience participation, create a one or two-page PDF handout with some key points. If you're feeling creative, make it a fill-in-the-blank format for people to follow along during the presentation. Not only will it encourage their participation, it fosters conversation and helps them to learn and implement solutions effectively.

REMIND YOUR GUESTS

Send a reminder email to everyone twenty-four hours before the event. Be sure to include the date, time, and location of the workshop! Express how excited you are to be delivering the content, and share how much you're looking forward to seeing them.

Be sure to send the reminder email to all who have been invited, even to those who may have originally declined. Those who initially couldn't attend may now be able to! Keep all doors open.

GETTING READY FOR THE EVENT

A few days before the workshop, decide what you will be wearing. You want to feel at ease and look polished, so choose something that is flattering but comfortable. Check if the outfit needs to be professionally cleaned or pressed.

Prepare your paperwork well in advance. Print yourself two copies of your presentation so you have a spare in case you misplace one while facilitating.

If you are feeling nervous, go ahead and read your notes out before hand and make any notes of specific points you want to touch on. Remember, your participants are genuinely interested in what you are doing!

Print out copies of your handouts and make sure to print extras in case someone wants to take an extra one home or share with a friend. Have your business cards available to be handed out. You may even want to paperclip a card to each handout.

Consider putting out a basket to collect names. In addition, perhaps you would like to offer a prize, discount, a freebie, or some tangible take-away / gift to those who've attended. Have fun with this, and let your creativity run wild!

THE EVENT

As guests arrive, I recommend approaching someone in advance to participate in your coaching demonstration. There are two reasons for this suggestion: first, this gives them the opportunity to prepare to participate; and second, it ensures you aren't awkwardly seeking a volunteer to fill a presentation gap.

Circulate a pen and paper requesting each participant's name, telephone number, and email address. Ensure that your sheet states you will email them from time to time.

When it comes time in your agenda to demonstrate a brief coaching experience, explain to everyone what they can expect. Get the "coachees" settled, and then explore a topic of their choice. Be sure to thank any volunteers for participating!

After the demonstration has been concluded, you can create a casual group discussion examining the experience. Again, have the rest of the audience recognize the coachee(s) for volunteering. Delve into your volunteers' experience: how did they feel, what insights were gained, and what will they take away from the experience?

Guests can be asked a couple of thought-provoking questions and ask them to offer any observations regarding the demonstration.

AFTER THE EVENT

Once the event is completed, congratulate yourself on a job well done!

Debrief your experience: What went well? What could have made it better? What are you proud of? These notes are for your eyes only, so don't censor yourself. You may review them before your next workshop, and it is important you make notes when everything is fresh in your mind.

Telephone each person who attended and thank them again for coming. This is an excellent opportunity to better understand their perspective of the event and receive feedback!

Be sure to ask:

» What did they find the most useful?

» Are they interested in becoming a client?

» Who do they know that they could recommend as a potential client or future workshop guest?

I highly recommend telephoning your guests rather than emailing. A voice-to-voice connection can be so much more powerful than one more message in their email box. At the same time, you get to practice asking for business which is a skill that needs to be practiced over and over to strengthen your sales muscle.

Remember each participant's contact information should later be included on your mailing list of prospective clients.

Don't forget to update your mailing list with all contact information gathered at the workshop so you can keep them apprised of future developments and events.

Action Checklist:

* 📌 **Determine target demographic.**

* 📌 **Establish interactive workshop topic.**

* 📌 **Decide how long your workshop with be.**

* 📌 **Determine date, time, and location to accommodate target audience.**

* 📌 **Create guest list.**

* 📌 **Issue invitations.**

* 📌 **Prepare presentation.**

* 📌 **Prepare paperwork, handouts, sign-up sheet.**

* 📌 **Send out reminders.**

* 📌 **Facilitate workshop.**

* 📌 **Ask for the business.**

* 📌 **Update your master contact list template.**

* 📌 **Celebrate your progress!**

* 📌 **Track your efforts.**

* 📌 **Schedule for follow-up as appropriate.**

STRATEGY #13:
DELIVER A SIGNATURE SPEECH

Delivering a signature speech that combines your expertise and coaching is an excellent approach to turbo-charge the growth of your business.

A well-crafted signature speech delivered to the right audience can be an impactful strategy simply by presenting to many people all at once! Whereas when you build your business exclusively through conducting one-on-one Sample Sessions, your reach is limited. There is only so much time in the day to set up the sessions, facilitate the experience, and follow up with potential clients.

Having exposure to a specifically targeted group immediately increases your reach! Combining your speech with an irresistible limited time offer is efficient *and* effective.

To best utilize this approach, there are three components to incorporate:

1. Create a well-designed, highly-targeted signature speech.

2. Find your specialized audience.

3. Include an irresistible offer.

DECIDE ON YOUR TOPIC

Ask yourself the following questions when deciding on your topic:

» "How does my expertise and experience specifically relate to the audience?"

» "What are the most pressing challenges my ideal client is experiencing?"

The answer to these questions will have a common ground, and that is the sweet spot for your signature speech topic! For example, you may be a coach who focuses on parenting, and you have four children; so, you have lots of personal experience in addition to your coach training.

If your audience has children transitioning from elementary to high school, they want to prepare them for a smooth transition.

Potential speech topics for those two factors could be:

» Ensuring Your Child Has a Great First Day at Their New School

» Bullyproof Your Child for High School

DRAFT YOUR SPEECH

We've all sat through a presentation in our lifetime that doesn't relate to our experience, and the speaker drones on and on.

Know your audience! Keep them engaged by sharing stories of experiences they can relate to and include interactive content. Position yourself to create an authentic connection and gain their trust.

What offer will you be including in your presentation? Be crystal clear about your offer, and reverse engineer your speech to ensure your presentation flows seamlessly.

A twenty-minute speech may seem daunting to create, but it really isn't that much content. It is approximately 2500 words, or five pages single spaced. The beauty of a twenty-minute speech is it can effortlessly be expanded to thirty minutes or reduced to fifteen minutes to accommodate your allotted time.

Here is a simple time outline for a twenty-minute speech:

→ Two-minute introduction (approximately 250 words)

→ Five minutes to cover Point #1 (approximately 625 words)

→ Five minutes to address Point #2 (approximately 625 words)

> →   Five minutes to discuss Point #3 (approximately 625 words)

> →   Three-minute conclusion (approximately 375 words)

Include a story to illustrate each of your three points. Everyone loves a story they can relate to, which in turn ensures they remember your presentation and your message! Clearly demonstrate specific results received through coaching to inspire them to act on your offer.

PREPARE AND REHEARSE

Rehearsing is a critical component of delivering a speech. Good preparation and practice helps confirm the length of your speech, at which point you can tailor it to maximize your time limit.

Transfer your speech onto cue cards or a short document that highlights the order of your presentation. When preparing your notes, use a large-scale font that you can easily glance at without losing momentum.

Not only do you want to read it aloud, you want to practice delivering it standing up, just as you will be before your audience. Practice speaking clearly, deliberately create eye contact with your audience, and consider your facial expressions and what you are doing with your body language.

Run through your delivery in front of a mirror; in front of your partner/spouse, children, and friends; even in front of your dog. You want to feel comfortable and have your speech become second nature, so the material feels completely routine.

When the time comes to deliver your speech, you don't want to read your presentation aloud. You will sound robotic and ridiculously sales-oriented. Practice a genuine delivery, and your audience will respond in kind.

CREATE A LIST OF POTENTIAL AUDIENCES

Brainstorm a list of local groups where your ideal clients gather. Many local groups are always on the lookout for guest presenters.

Research the groups before approaching them, analyzing the following:

» What is the group's mission?

» What types of presentations have they had in the past?

» What are the topics of discussion?

Find the name and contact information of the program coordinator, and reach out to them directly. Don't hesitate to share the expertise you have and how you can benefit their members.

Start with smaller groups to practice and hone your speech. You'll gain confidence with each delivery and can work your way to delivering for more prominent groups.

In addition to local speaking opportunities, many organizations have virtual speaking platforms and national conferences. You'll be amazed by the potential opportunities that arise simply by asking!

PERSONALIZE EACH APPROACH

Personalize your approach to each specific group. You will have more success with a personalized approach to a couple of well-researched groups than with a mass market approach.

Address your proposal to one specific individual, explaining who you are, what you do, and most importantly, the value you can offer to the members of their group. Incorporate the information gathered during your research to show them you are knowledgeable and are capable in the benefit you can provide to their people.

Do not send a mass email with the same presentation proposal copy-and-pasted to each organization.

A few days after you have submitted your presentation email, follow up with a telephone call and offer to meet to discuss how you can support their goals.

DELIVERING YOUR SPEECH

The day of your speech, you will understandably be nervous. This feeling may present as a rush of adrenaline which will have you short of breath and talking really *really* quickly. Before you step in front of the crowd, take the opportunity to take a couple of very deep breaths. You may also want to take a moment and assume a power pose position: standing in a wide stance with arms perched on your hips and chin in the air! You may feel silly, so take the opportunity in a washroom and outside of your audience's line of sight.

There is a lot of psychology behind the success of assuming the superhero power pose before public speaking. Studies have shown that assuming the superhero power pose for two minutes before making a presentation has results that may surprise you! Levels of testosterone dramatically surge, and levels of cortisol drops. Cortisol is considered one of the "stress hormones" and is a big influence of the "fight-or-flight" response. By increasing our testosterone and reducing our cortisol levels, we increase our ability for abstract thinking, we have a higher discomfort threshold, and we are more likely to take risks.

Two minutes of the superhero power pose is a wise investment to a presentation delivered well!

When you take centre stage, don't worry if you see audience members check their phone. It's easy to assume that you must be boring them, but it probably has nothing to do with you. Smile, speak clearly, and make eye contact with your audience. Be sure to look at a variety of audience members so no one audience member feels they are being stared down.

The more comfortable you feel, the more comfortable your audience will be. People can sense uptight, nervous, fretful energy, and they will instantly question your expert authority.

At the end of your speech, ensure you have a way to gather names and email addresses, and collect business cards if available. You may want to consider offering a drawing as a natural way of collecting the contact information.

If you have received permission in advance, you can also add them to your master email list for future follow-up.

In addition, use LinkedIn and/or your preferred social media platform to reach out to each individual who attended. Begin to establish a relationship with everyone so in the future you can invite them to participate in a Sample Session.

Action Checklist:

- 📌 **Determine your target audience.**

- 📌 **Decide on potential topic.**

- 📌 **List local groups that could benefit from a presentation.**

- 📌 **Create personalized pitch to groups.**

- Track your efforts and schedule for follow-up.

- Create a specialized and irresistible offer.

- Draft your speech around the specialized offer.

- Prepare and rehearse.

- Deliver speech.

- Collect contact information.

- Update your master contact list.

- Send "thank you" note to the group coordinator.

- Celebrate your progress!

- Follow up for feedback.

- Reach out to participants via LinkedIn or other social media.

- Track all communication.

- Schedule for follow-up as appropriate.

STRATEGY #14:
ORGANIZE A PUBLIC EVENT

You've likely noticed that the suggested strategies are becoming bolder! Right about now you may be thinking, "A public event! Are you nuts?! I could never do something like that!"

But if you have stuck with me this far, bear with me as I explore this idea. While intimidating at first, you may find it is a perfect strategy for you.

If you created a mini workshop as recommended in Strategy #12, organizing a public event is the natural evolution.

The ultimate purpose of holding a public event is to grow your client base and promote your business.

The beauty of a public event is twofold: one, you can invite those already in your circle and existing mailing list, and two, it is open to the public. The event should be open to anyone who registers, and if you have attracted their attention, there is a definite interest in what you're presenting!

It continues to establish yourself as an accessible resource, an expert on the subject, and a natural leader within your sector.

Holding public events have never been easier, and there is a wide range of resources to help you organize and promote your event for little or no cost.

CLARIFY YOUR OBJECTIVE

Some ideas for your consideration are:

» Will this be a one-time event, or will it be a series of networking events?

» How can you repurpose content from your workshop or signature speech?

» Will you have a guest presenter?

» Where is an accessible location for your event?

» When is your preferred audience's optimum time to be able to attend?

Be clear on your goal. If you are looking to grow your coaching practice, keep the cost reasonable for your audience. However, if you are looking to expand your services into group coaching programs and/or online digital courses, consider holding multiple events and utilize these public events to generate a steady stream of diverse income.

INVITING A GUEST PRESENTER

If you invite a guest presenter, ensure it is someone who also assists your ideal client but doesn't encroach upon the services you provide.

Having a guest speaker positions you to exchange and receive referrals with them. This is a natural way of expanding your Business Referral Network from Strategy #8. This approach makes you the natural go-to resource for both your referral partner and your potential clients.

In addition, having a guest presenter shows you collaborate with others well and exert influence within the sector, further positioning you as an expert and leader.

Another advantage to having a guest presenter is it reduces the amount of preparation and content development you must do yourself.

For example, if you are a business coach your guest could be a business law specialist or expert in negotiation skills, marketing, or financing.

When inviting a guest presenter, be very clear with them about your expectations. Here are some points to help initiate dialogue about collaborating:

» Why do you want the guest speaker to work with you?

» What is your goal?

» Do you want a presentation that is thirty minutes with handouts? Or are you looking for a hands-on demonstration for the audience?

» Are they able to sell at the event? Or do you only want them to deliver useful information?

» Will there be time for a question-and-answer period after their presentation?

» Do you expect the presenter to provide a written introduction for you to introduce them?

» Will you be paying the presenter an honorarium, and if so how much?

» Do you expect the presenter to assist you in promoting the event and invite their own circle and mailing lists?

» Can the presenter collect names for solicitation?

» Will there only be one email sign-up sheet that your guest presenter will also have access to?

» Request that you have a copy of their presentation agenda no later than one week prior to the event for approval.

» Ask the guest presenter to record a practice session and forward it to you in advance, as well as any documentation or handouts they will be using.

» Decide on a dress rehearsal that both you and the guest presenter can attend.

» Will your guest presenter be interested in offering an incentive giveaway, drawing, or door prize?

SELECTING LOCATION

Choose a central location that is easily accessible by transit and has ample parking.

The size of the location will dictate the number of tickets you can sell, but begin with a smaller location to test the waters. If it is a success and you enjoy coordinating these events, you can always expand in size and complexity in the future.

Be sure to visit the venue in person before finalizing the booking.

There is nothing worse than booking a meeting room only to find out there is no Wi-fi for your presentation, or there aren't enough tables or chairs, or that the washrooms are a five-minute hike from the meeting area.

Visiting the location beforehand gives you an advantage in your preparation, will save you stress, and help ensure your event runs smoothly with minimal disruptions.

This way you know what it looks like for your own set-up preparations.

DATE, TIME, DURATION, AND COST

Your preferred audience and their availability will naturally dictate the date and time of your event, just as it did with your workshop.

When you book the space, ensure that you also have access to accommodate setting up. You will also want to have at least an additional thirty minutes before guests are to arrive in case you have early birds or encounter any complications. Having a buffer zone will help you to be calm comfortable and reduce any potential stress.

Refer to Strategy #12—Hosting a Workshop—to help you create content for your event.

Prepare your agenda well in advance. Practice your presentation so it is seamless.

If you are including a guest speaker, ask to see their presentation a week before the event. Ensure it matches your expectations and the needs of your guests.

It is reasonable for you to charge enough to cover your expenses and perhaps create income in exchange for your time and coordination efforts.

PREPARATION

Prepare your agenda well in advance and practice it so your delivery is as seamless as possible. Create an itinerary that can be presented to guests as they arrive.

Make sure you have a way to gather contact information from attendees. You will probably receive a list of emails from the registration, but always be proactive and have a sign-up sheet as well as a jar to collect business cards.

Consider giving out swag or door prizes.

Remember: the success of your event hinges on the attendees' experiences. If they think they are coming to see a presentation on a particular topic, they expect that is what they will be hearing. Ensure they are getting what they expect. Your reputation depends on it!

CREATING A DESCRIPTIVE WRITE-UP

Describe your event and clearly identify your target audience. Describe why they would want to attend the event, explain what they will learn, and inform them as to what they will take away from the experience.

Be sure to include the exact address of the location and any necessary directions.

Identify any equipment or supplies they will need to bring with them, and clearly state what will be provided.

Will there be any refreshments available? For example, will there be complimentary tea and light refreshments? Or perhaps there will be a cash bar or on-site vendor to purchase their lunch?

Since you don't know where your guests are coming from, this helps them to prepare and ensures they have a positive experience.

PROMOTING THE EVENT

Post your event on all your social media platforms, and send a notification to everyone on your email list.

Consider creating a Facebook event, being sure that the privacy settings are set as public so the information can be widely shared.

Ask your friends and guest presenters to please share the posts on your behalf. The more you can expand your reach, the better your attendance will be.

Utilize resources—such as Meetup or Eventbrite—to help you organize and promote your event for little or no cost. Meetup is a huge network, and millions of people are using it to grow their businesses, including coaches just like you. These social media platforms will promote the event on your behalf and broaden your list of participants.

RECRUIT AN ASSISTANT

Ask someone to be your assistant for the day of the event.

Typically, your assistant attends the event for free in exchange for supporting you throughout the day.

Your assistant will help with logistics, such as setting up tables and seating, preparing refreshments, welcoming and registering the attendees, and collecting contact information.

An extra set of hands can be a lifesaver if something goes wrong. It is also helpful to have someone assist in keeping your guests comfortable.

MONITOR YOUR SIGN-UPS

How many people have signed up a week before the event? Forty-eight hours beforehand? Twenty-four hours beforehand?

It is common for people to wait until the last day to sign up, as well as for those who sign up early not to appear. When you are aware of these natural inclinations, you won't be stressed if everyone you thought would attend doesn't end up making it.

DRESS REHEARSAL

The day before the event, you will want to do a rehearsal of the agenda with the presenters and speakers. Ensure everyone has their presentations and handouts prepared. If the space is not available, host a video conference to rehearse to ensure a smooth-flowing presentation.

It is crucial that the agenda be run through prior to the event itself to ensure easy flow.

EVENT DAY

Gather all your supplies, content, handouts, itinerary, and registration information. Arrive at your venue early in case any guests arrive early, as well as to ensure proper set-up.

Lean on your assistant for support so you can spend time connecting with the attendees as they arrive. This is an excellent time to initiate and invest in establishing relationships.

Adhere to your agenda and start on time out of respect to all attending. Although some may arrive late, it is important for you to honour those who arrived at the appointed time.

AFTER THE EVENT

Gratitude is an important part of cultivating relationships.

Be sure to send a "thank you" note to all who attended, of course including your guest presenters.

Send your assistant a small gift as an extra "thank you."

How you follow up is important to nurture relationships and maintain communication with your people.

If you plan future events, let the attendees know and be sure to send them a personal invitation. You could also create a VIP list of past attendees and perhaps offer them a future discount, special bonus, or front-of-the-line access to future events.

Action Checklist:

- Download the free sheet for calculating overhead.

- Clarity your event objective.

- Incorporate workshop and speech content.

- Create agenda.

- Approach guest presenter.

- Communicate clearly your expectations and contributions from guest presenter.

- Decide on accessible location.

- Establish date, time, duration, and cost.

https://bit.ly/2MDhoql

- ★ **Create descriptive write-up.**

- ★ **Actively promote the event date.**

- ★ **Recruit an assistant.**

- ★ **Monitor your sign-ups.**

- ★ **Track all communication.**

- ★ **Schedule for follow-up event reminder.**

- ★ **Have dress rehearsal.**

- ★ **Facilitate event.**

- ★ **Collect contact information.**

- ★ **Update master contact list.**

- ★ **Reach out to participants via LinkedIn or other social media.**

- ★ **Send "thank you" notes to assistant and guest presenter.**

- ★ **Schedule follow up.**

- ★ **Celebrate your progress!**

STRATEGY #15:
BECOME THE KIND OF COACH YOU YOURSELF WOULD HIRE

The first fourteen strategies are practical, step-by-step approaches, and these are highly effective ways of building your business. This final strategy—to become the kind of coach you yourself would hire—will add rocket fuel to the first fourteen.

One of the best ways to get clients is to show up powerfully in the world. This means walking your walk, talking your talk, and truly living in alignment with your values, your higher self, and at the highest level of integrity.

People who embody these qualities truly do stand out. They are the people who shine and inspire us to live more fully. To attract the clients you want, you've got to become the coach you'd want to hire.

This means being committed to your personal growth. This is courageous work—to be continually pressing the envelope on your personal evolution.

So how do you do this? Start with a daily practice in personal development. It might be through journaling, prayer, meditation, or inspirational reading. Continue to learn and attend training sessions and workshops that will help you upgrade your self-awareness and your skills.

Hire your own coaches. Yes, you read that right! I recommend engaging more than one coach. The most successful coaches have multiple coaches. Each coach has a unique speciality and perspective, so focus on hiring a specialist for your personal development, another for your business, and perhaps a third in another area in which you want to excel. When you invest in yourself, you will see the pay-off in your personal fulfillment which will lead to quantum results in your business.

Each day add value consistently by how you live your life. Be active, helpful, and generously contribute to your community through service.

CONCLUSION

Once I made the non-negotiable commitment to get more clients *and* I was ready to receive them, there was no stopping me!

That's how I know, that in addition to supporting hundreds of aspiring coaches, by far *the most important mindset shift* to successfully fill your practice with paying clients is: the decision to do so! To confidently declare yourself ready and willing to receive them!

When you become open and determined to receive new clients, the Universe conspires to support you and coincidences will begin to flow. The right clients will show up, and when they do, you have a tangible action plan!

Be grateful and express your gratitude.

Invite others to a Sample Session, and coach them like you mean it. Even the newest coaches bring enormous value by *sincerely listening* to their clients. That is the true power of connection: validating another's experience.

Help them feel supported and empower them with the knowing they can overcome their challenges!

Now that you have finished this book, go back to the strategies section and identify which seem the most natural fit to you. Commit to practising your chosen strategies for at least three months, and track as you go.

Embed the strategies into your practice and make them a second nature habit before giving up and trying something else. Consistency is the biggest predictor of success. There is no quick fix, no one-size-fits-all strategy. If you're not getting stellar results after the first week, be prepared to stick with it. Look for the small gains and celebrate them!

With every action you consistently undertake, you are making progress!

Lastly, remind yourself you are learning how to build a business, and it takes time to become masterful at any new skill. There are people less qualified than you, doing the things they want to do, simply because they decided to believe in themselves. Period.

Make the decision to get out of your own way.

Here's to your success!

ABOUT THE AUTHOR

Human BEING, wife, mother, family member, friend, nature lover, dancer, dreamer, barefoot leader, authentic introvert, sacred rebel, joy seeker.

Candy is trained as an engineer and has held every level of job from entry level, through to senior corporate director for one of the largest real estate management companies worldwide. She leverages this real-world experience with her coaching clients.

She holds coaching credentials from the International Coaching Federation and was trained at the Harvard of coach training, The Coaches Training Institute. Her clients are women and men from all walks of life, with this common thread: they want a better life and a better business. They know the fastest way to get it is through coaching and mentoring.

She work with brilliant people to create a breakthrough in skills and mindset, significantly improving their satisfaction, performance and results. At the heart of her work is a passion for empowering people to reach their full potential. She supports entrepreneurs to understand who they are at their best and get clear on blind spots that impede their success, so they can thrive.

As a highly sought-after business coach, consultant and public speaker she frequently shares her proven strategies and cutting-edge tactics with people internationally.

She works with clients one-on-one, in groups and through online resources and programs.

She can be contacted directly by email at info@candymotzek.com

Visit her at **stepintosuccessnow.com** to get books, courses and other training materials as well as many FREE resources on how to start and build your thriving business.